Botaniphoria

Having grown up with nature books and frequent visits to the parks and gardens in her hometown, Kyoto, Japan, Asuka Hishiki has always been fascinated by nature, drawn to portray the plants and wildlife surrounding her. After completing her Masters degree at Kyoto City University of Arts, she spent 10 years in New York City delving more into her artistic style. Her work spans drawings of rare, endangered species to more familiar vegetables found in the home, vividly painted in astonishing detail. For the past decade, it has addressed environmental issues and the survival of the natural world, including large-scale installations using recycled paper on the migratory patterns of monarch butterflies. She has also participated in residencies at renowned botanical gardens around the world as part of a decades-long initiative to produce vast visual records (florilegia) of contemporary botanical collections.

Work held

The Huntington Library, Art Museum, and Botanical Gardens, CA, USA
Royal Botanic Gardens, Kew, London, UK
Hunt institute for Botanical Documentation, PA, USA
Shirley Sherwood Collection, London, UK
Denver Botanic Gardens, CO, USA
National Tropical Botanical Garden, Hawaii, USA
New York State Museum, NY, USA
The Horticultural Society of New York, NY, USA
Singapore Botanic Gardens, Singapore

For recent works, upcoming show schedules and exhibiting history, please visit her website at greenasas.com or find her on Instagram @greenasas.

Botanical Art Portfolios

The Whole Story: Painting more than just the flowers by Christina Hart-Davies
Botanical Artistry: Plants, projects & processes by Julia Trickey

Botanical Art Portfolios is a new series featuring distinguished botanical artists, their work and their inspiration. Intentionally both beautiful and useful, these handy-sized paperbacks are designed to be taken anywhere, referred to, collected and gazed at. Each book will bring out the personality of its individual artist, showcase their work and share why they love what they do, explain their choice of subjects, the distinct techniques they have developed, and their failures as well as their successes.

See http://tworiverspress.com/botanical_art_portfolios for more information.

Also published by Two Rivers Press

Islamic Art Meets British Flowers by Hadil Tamim and Adrian Lawson
The Greenwood Trees: History, folklore and uses of Britain's trees by Christina Hart-Davies
Reading Abbey and the Abbey Quarter by Peter Durrant and John Painter
Reading's Bayeux Tapestry by Reading Museum
A Wild Plant Year: History, folklore and uses of Britain's flora by Christina Hart-Davies
Silchester: Life on the Dig by Jenny Halstead & Michael Fulford
Caught on Camera: Reading in the 70s by Terry Allsop
Plant Portraits by Post: Post & Go British Flora by Julia Trickey
Allen W. Seaby: Art and Nature by Martin Andrews & Robert Gillmor
Cover Birds by Robert Gillmor
An Artist's Year in the Harris Garden by Jenny Halstead
Caversham Court Gardens: A Heritage Guide by Friends of Caversham Court Gardens
Birds, Blocks & Stamps: Post & Go Birds of Britain by Robert Gillmor
Down by the River: The Thames and Kennet in Reading by Gillian Clark

Botaniphoria

A Cabinet of Botanical Curiosities

Asuka Hishiki

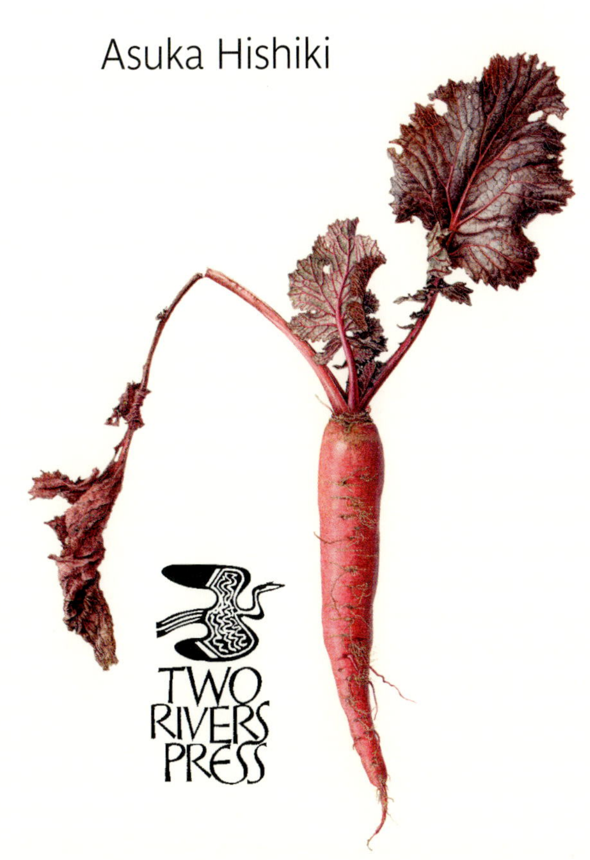

Red daikon (2021)

TWO RIVERS PRESS

First published in the UK in 2023 by Two Rivers Press
7 Denmark Road, Reading RG1 5PA
www.tworiverspress.com

ISBN 978-1-915048-10-3

2 3 4 5 6 7 8 9

Two Rivers Press is represented in the UK by Inpress Ltd
and distributed by BookSource, Glasgow.

Cover painting by Asuka Hishiki
'A portrait of a heirloom tomato: Sexy lady' (2021). Watercolour on paper, 10 × 11½ in

Cover design by Nadja Robinson

Inside cover artwork by Asuka Hishiki
'Red list wallpaper Kyoto 2015' (2021). Installation/inkjet print

Text design by Nadja Robinson and typeset in Parisine

Printed and bound in Great Britain by Short Run Press, Exeter

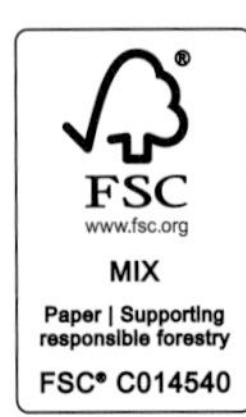

Acknowledgements

First of all, I would like to thank the amazing Two Rivers Press team. Thank you Sally, Nadja and Anne for the thoughtful and generous care you gave to me and the book. Without your professional and talented help, I would have been in the dark. It was a simple pleasure to work with you!

I thank Julia for taking me on this wonderful journey. Until she suggested making a book, it never came to my mind. Thanks to her kind smile and gentle guidance, my adventure was so joyful.

Of course, I would like to thank all my friends who are always there for me–who shared their wisdom with me, who gave me generous suggestions, who invariably inspired me. You all make my life rich and better.

Also, I would like to thank my farmer and gardener friends who generously shared their breathtaking subjects and passion for growing.

Lastly, I thank my mother, Setsuko and my father Masaaki, and all of my family who have encouraged me to keep my dream going since I was small. And my partner, Masanobu, who is my biggest supporter, best friend and always has my back.

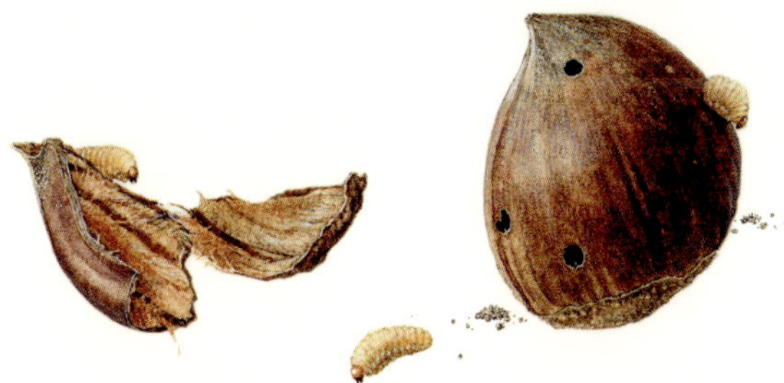

Turezure no kusa:
A chestnut and
chestnut worms (2018)

Contents

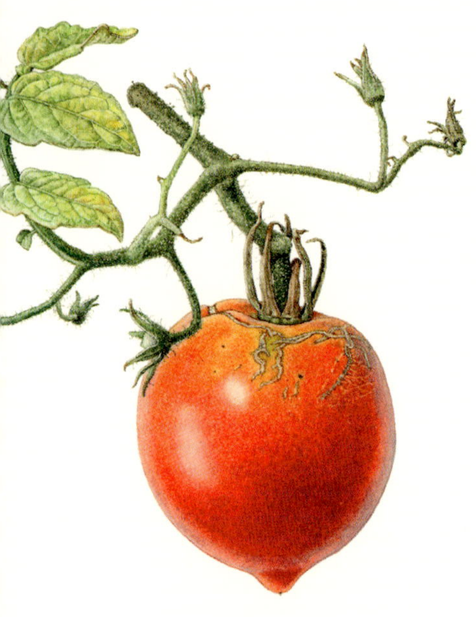

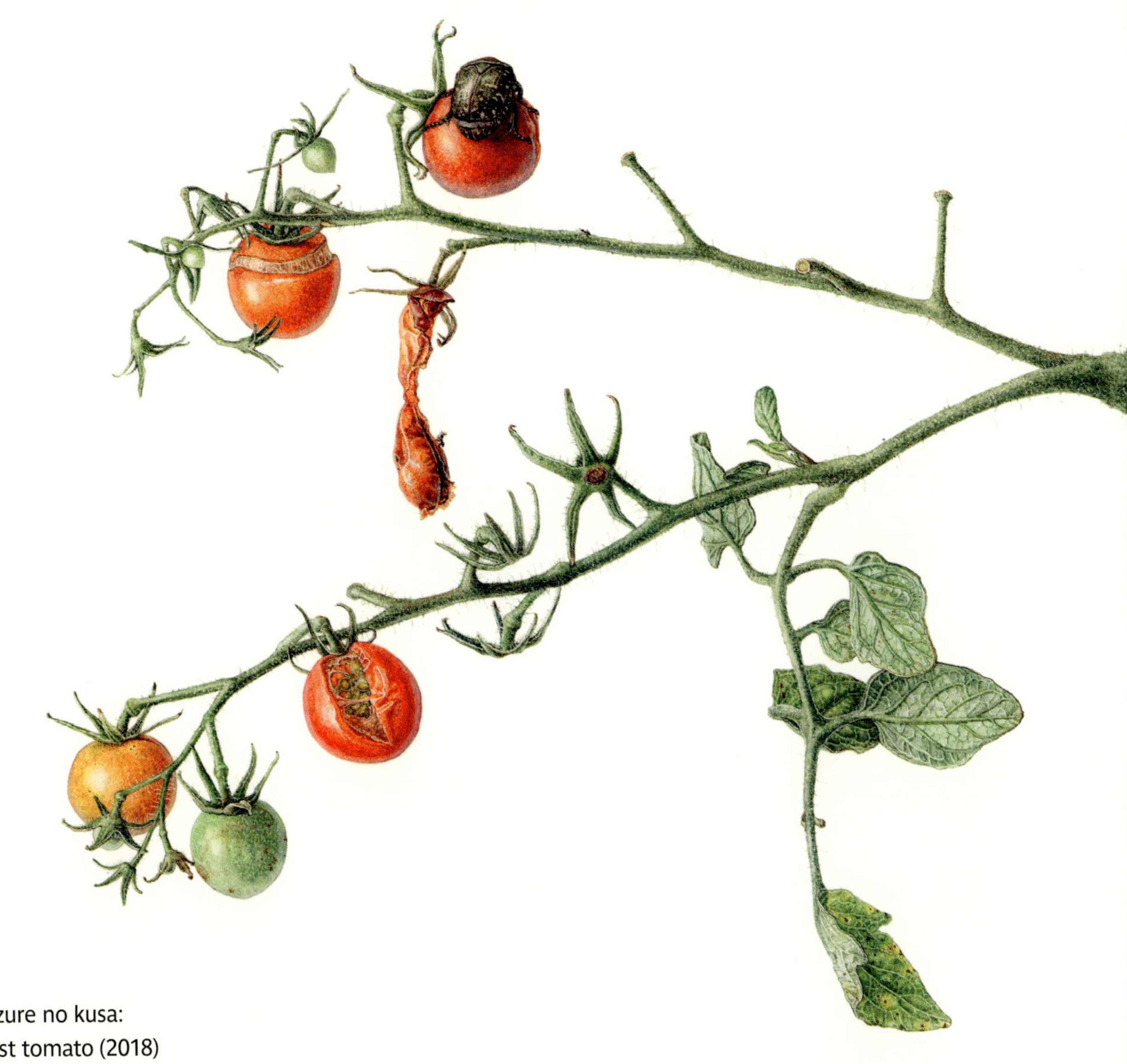

Turezure no kusa:
Breast tomato (2018)

Turezure no kusa:
After long rain tomato (2021)

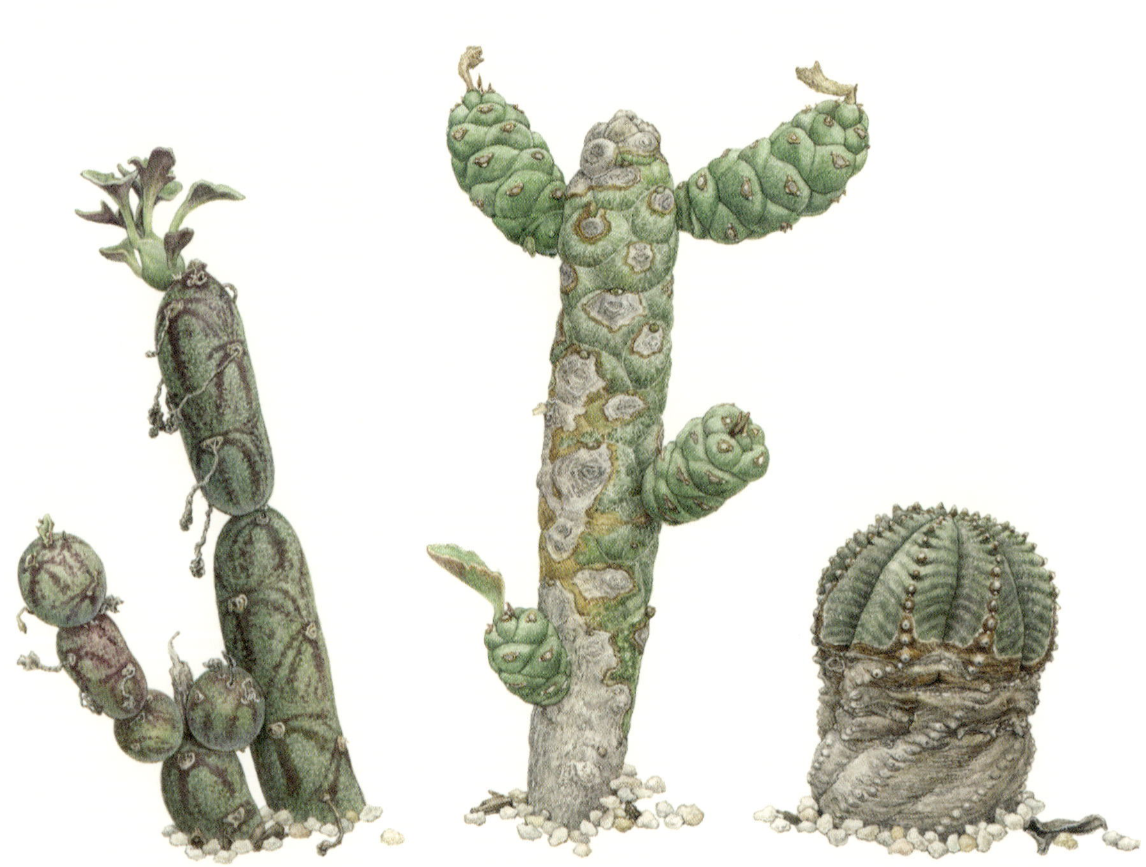

Botaniphoria

Ever since I was a small child, I've liked two things: to paint and to flip through the pages of illustrated books of insects, plants and animals. Until I learnt that scholars took painters with them on their research trips around the world centuries ago, I never thought to connect the two. Then I immediately thought how wonderful it would be if I could spend my days travelling around the world drawing plants and insects. However, instead of going out on adventures and finding exciting new species, I found beauty in ordinary vegetables and weeds on the street. A common butterfly in my backyard became much more valuable than a rare, undiscovered species to me.

Nature pleases not only my eyes, it inspires me in various ways. I wonder, I get curious and I am amazed. If I see something interesting, my imagination flies like a butterfly. At the same time, it makes me worry, because we are facing many, many environmental problems. I have come to understand that I know very little about these issues, and it is sad to think that this beautiful day today doesn't last any longer than it does. However, it is even sadder to imagine that a common butterfly may not be flying in our backyard for future generations to enjoy, perhaps becoming a rare endangered species. These thoughts and worries are woven into my artworks, but my main motivation in creating them is to share the beauty of nature and celebrate the simple joy of experiencing it.

How can I articulate my feelings when I find a treasure? It's excitement and euphoria, which is like being hit by lightning or falling in love. The treasure itself is often overlooked as an insignificant piece of nature. For example, a half-rotten tomato, a mundane acorn, a broken or crumpled

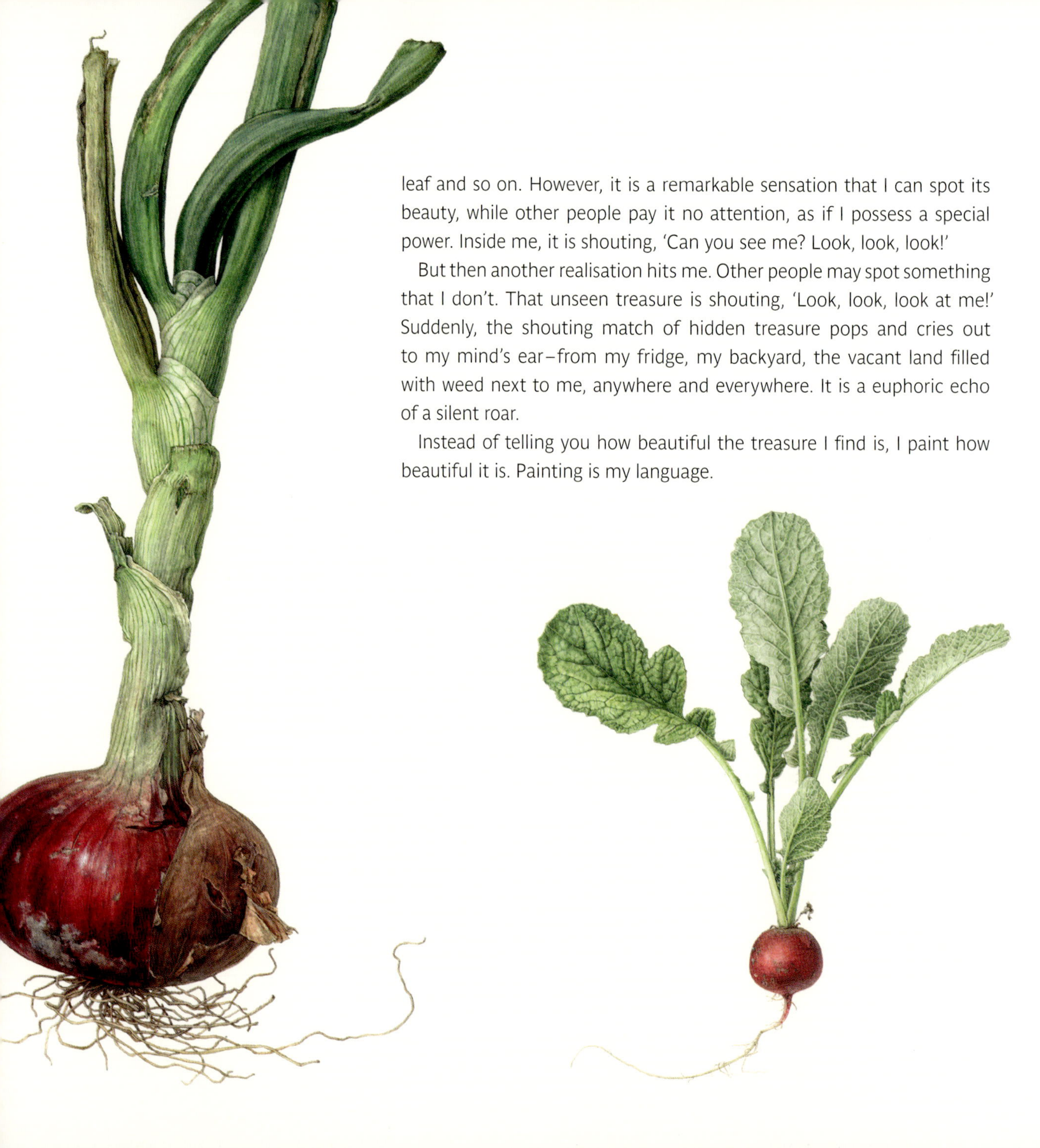

leaf and so on. However, it is a remarkable sensation that I can spot its beauty, while other people pay it no attention, as if I possess a special power. Inside me, it is shouting, 'Can you see me? Look, look, look!'

But then another realisation hits me. Other people may spot something that I don't. That unseen treasure is shouting, 'Look, look, look at me!' Suddenly, the shouting match of hidden treasure pops and cries out to my mind's ear–from my fridge, my backyard, the vacant land filled with weed next to me, anywhere and everywhere. It is a euphoric echo of a silent roar.

Instead of telling you how beautiful the treasure I find is, I paint how beautiful it is. Painting is my language.

Asuka in Wonderland

When I first landed in New York City, I knew no one and I didn't speak English. It was like falling into a rabbit hole. The city was a fascinating but bizarre place, where my common sense didn't feel normal. I felt like Alice in Wonderland, immersed in an eccentric life. We will skip the details of my adventures since, looking back now, these were not so extraordinary – probably because I got used to the 'eccentricities' or because the world had changed. Everything moves so fast these days.

My life in New York City affected my art strongly. Just walking through the city, public art was everywhere, and concerts and performances were happening at subway stations. I shouldn't forget to mention the many, many museums, galleries, events, parks, farmers' markets and, of course, meeting interesting people. Inspiration came from everywhere, but it almost became too much at one point, so I tried staying home to work on my own. Yet my life wasn't an easy one. Like Alice's story, the mean Queen of Hearts was yelling and screaming orders that I felt forced to follow. And just like the Mad Hatter's tea party, I didn't have any idea what they were talking about.

But I met a blue caterpillar on a mushroom, who talked to me. He was one of the very first clients who bought my artwork. He said: 'Your work is not for hanging on the wall in a bright living room; instead it is for putting in a drawer in the study. Then, in the middle of the night, one can come down to the study alone, take out your artwork and ponder over it. That kind of artwork.'

I am not sure how much I understood the wisdom of the wonderland, but this was the best compliment I was given.

Now, I have moved back to Japan. Our place is not located in a busy city, nor nature-rich countryside, but in between. I spend surprisingly calm days there compared to my life in New York City, just painting all

Purple onion (2011)

Allium cepa

Radish (2018)

Raphanus raphanistrum
subsp. *sativus*

day, cooking meals and talking to myself, my partner and his cats. But still, my interest in nature hasn't changed. Throughout my adventures, including my youth, my fascination is always about it. And in this fast, rapidly moving world, some things stay unchanged – everything I use is borrowed from history. I still use watercolour on paper. I still use a live subject and my theme is 'good old nature'.

When I was invited to produce this book, I started selecting my works and seeking fragments of my thoughts and memories to connect them all together. I was excited because it is like having a solo exhibition on your bookshelf, the show you can visit whenever you wish. Then the wisdom of the blue caterpillar came back to me. So I sincerely hope, in the middle of a sleepless night, instead of switching on your phone, you will open this book and ponder over it.

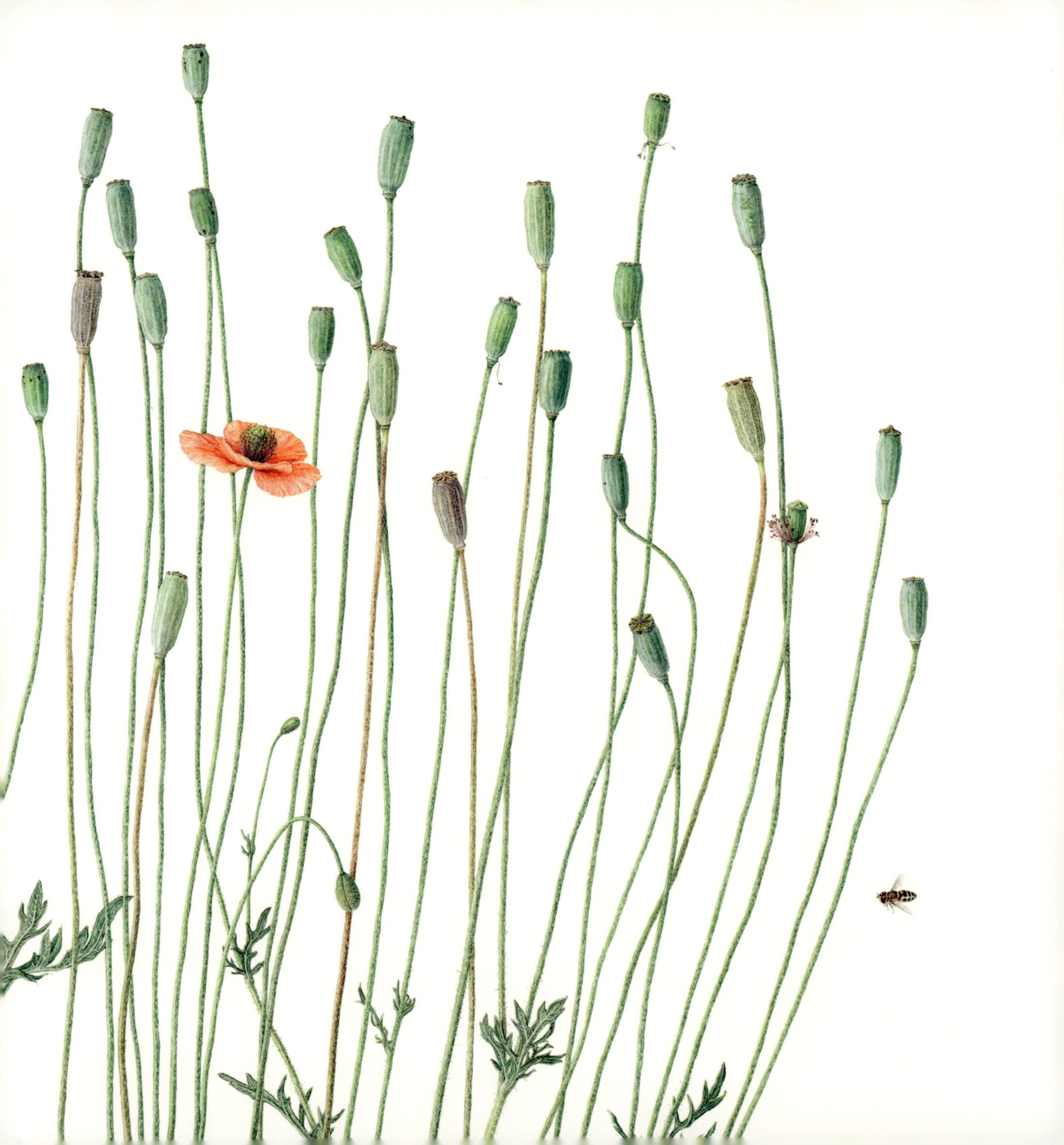

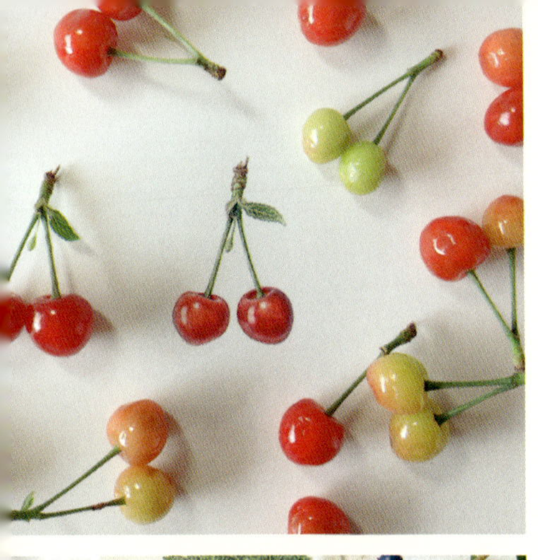
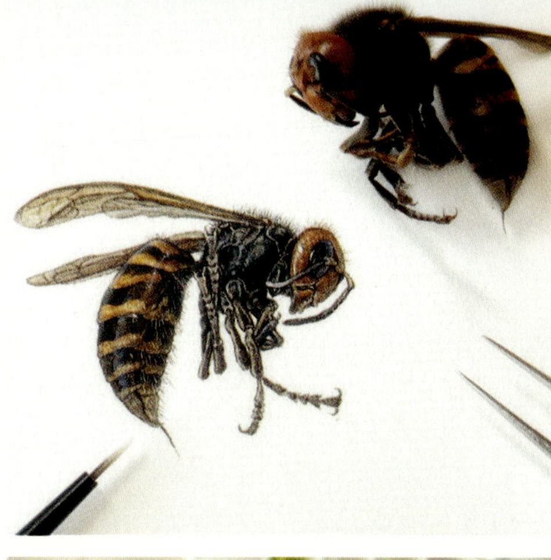
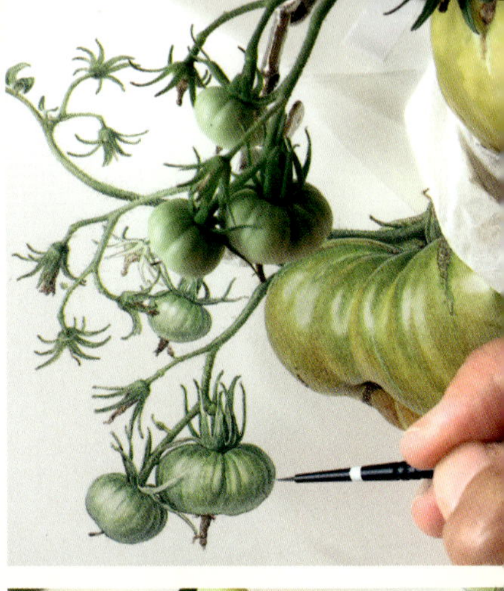
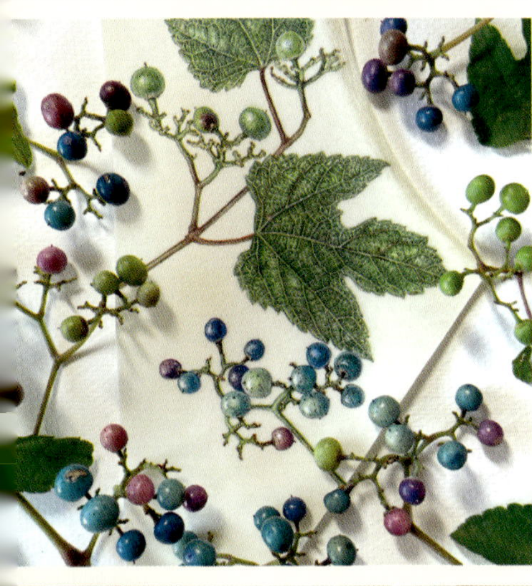
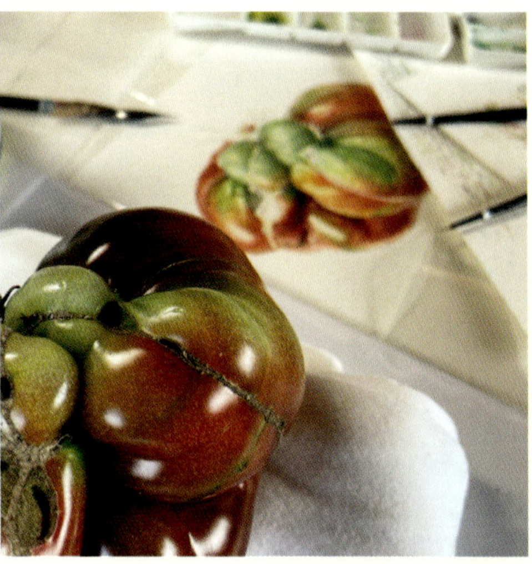
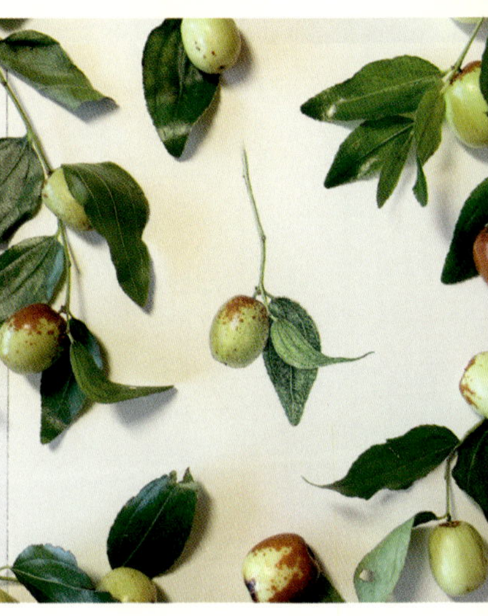
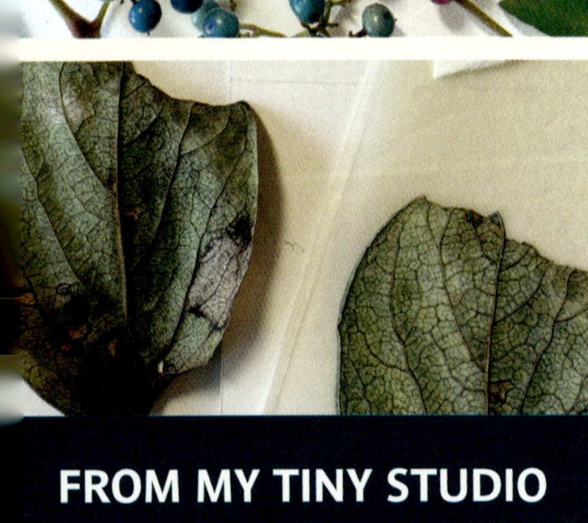
FROM MY TINY STUDIO
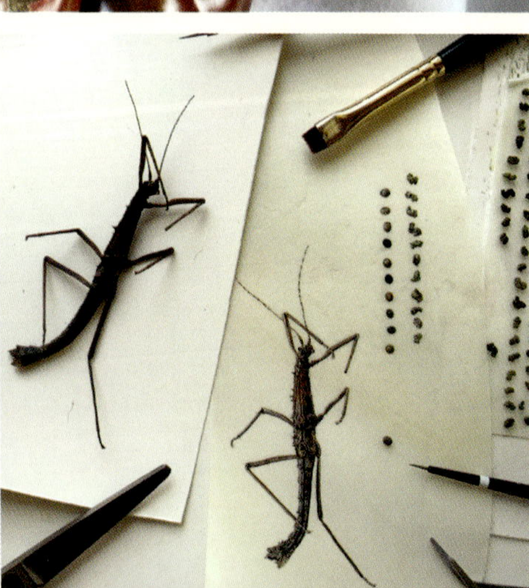
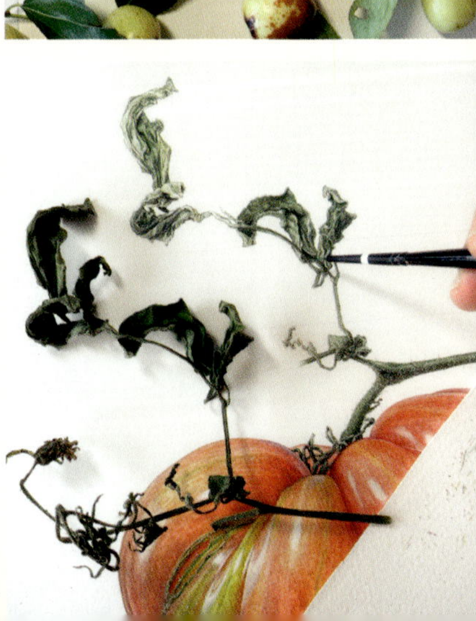

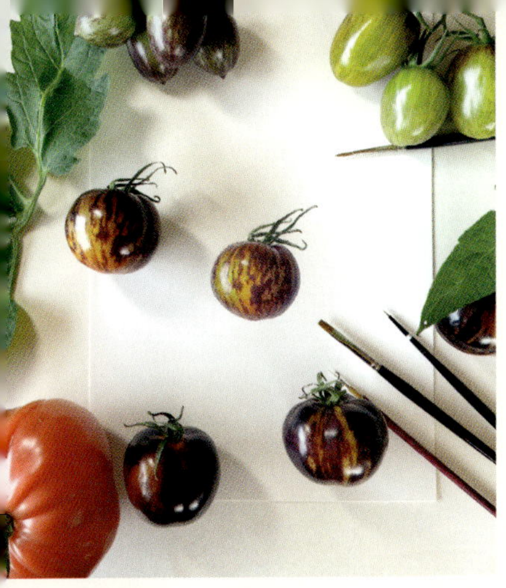

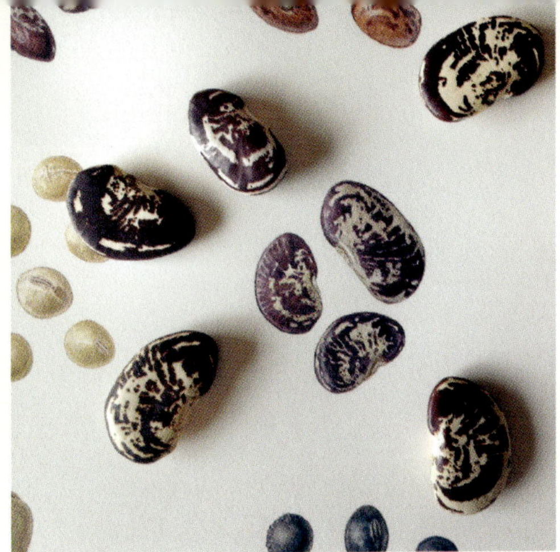

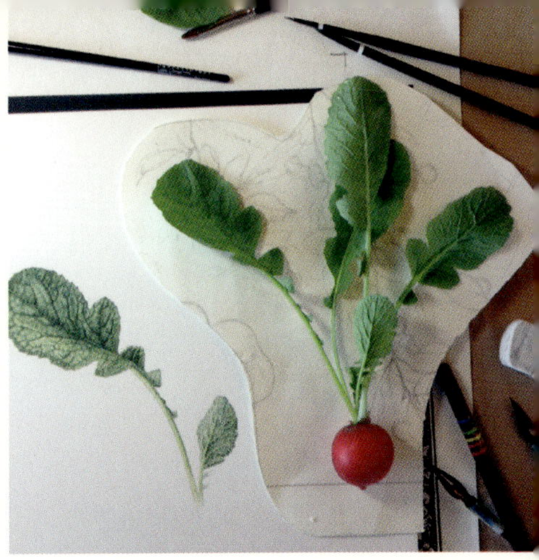

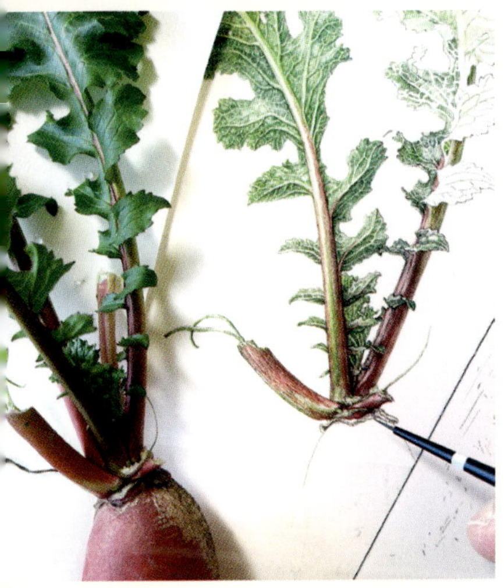

SUBJECT MATTERS
Working with live subjects

Working with live subjects is chaotic. So, here I would like to share some photos of the subjects alongside my images. The two objects look alike at first but then diverge along different paths. One lives for ever and the other decomposes and returns to Mother Earth!

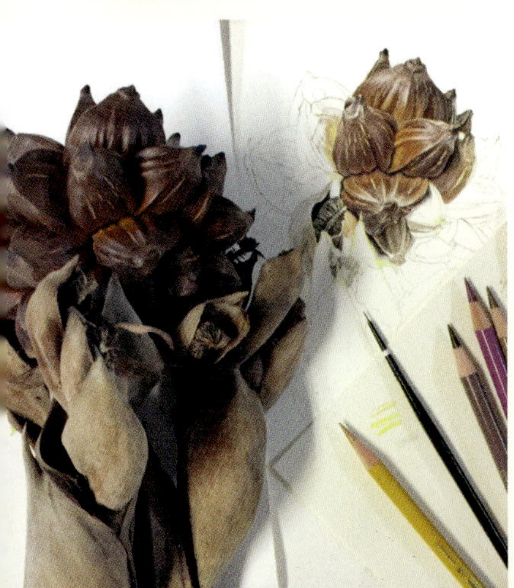

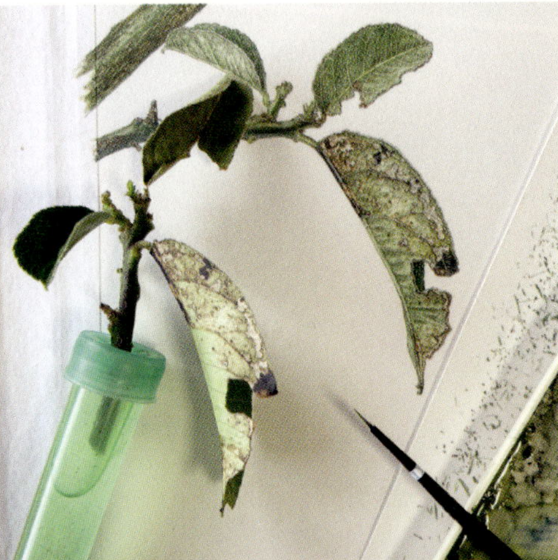

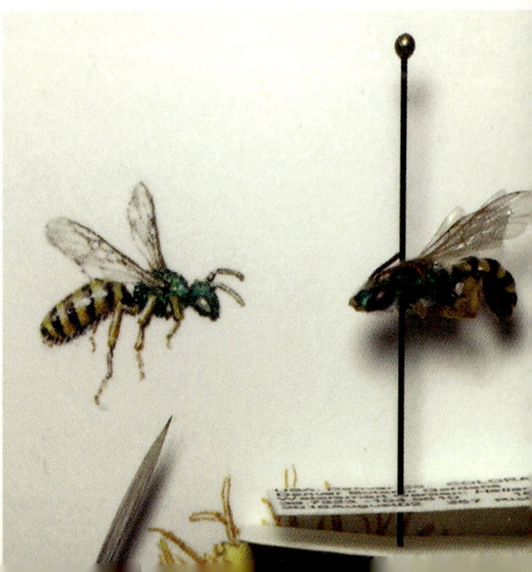

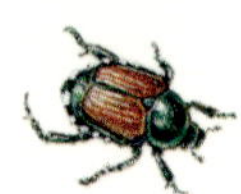
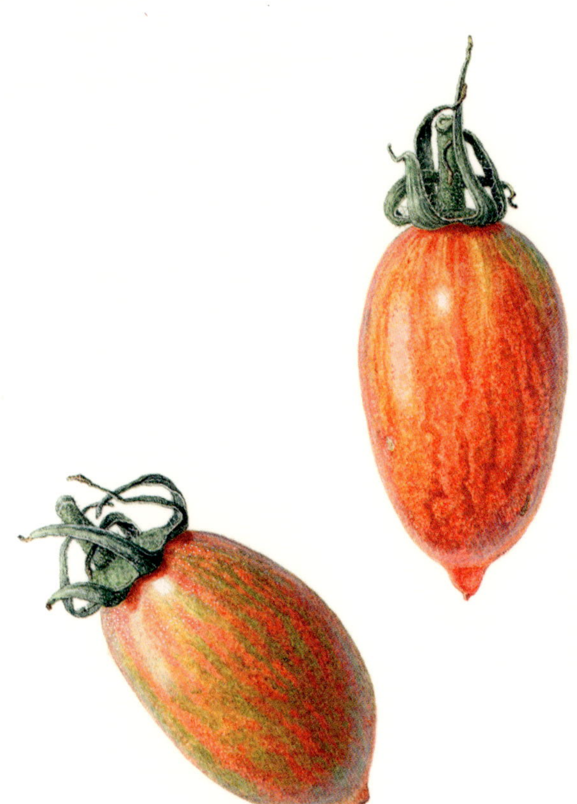
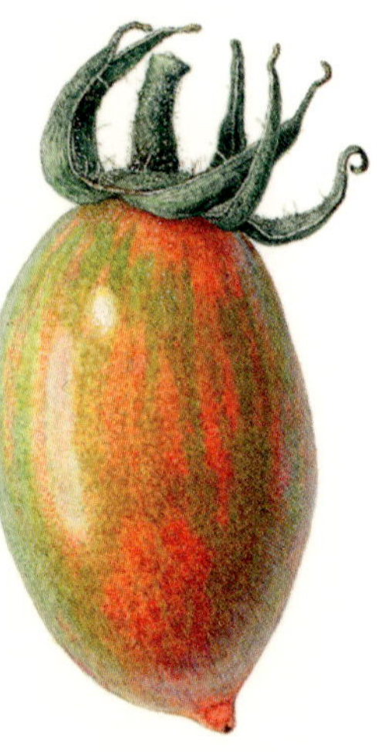

I. Botanical alchemy

Jewels and treasures in your kitchen and backyard

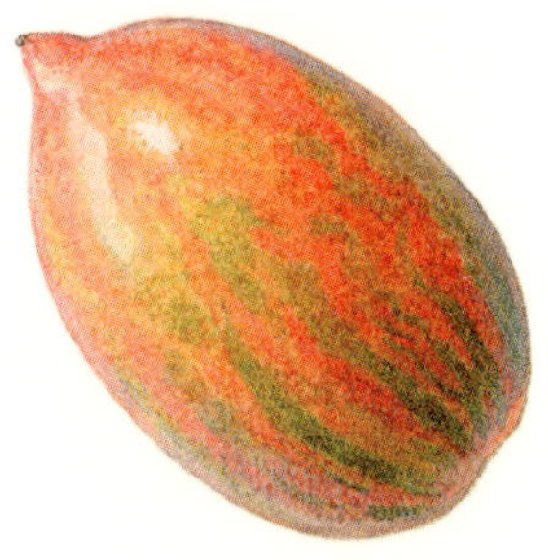

Jewel tomatoes (2022)

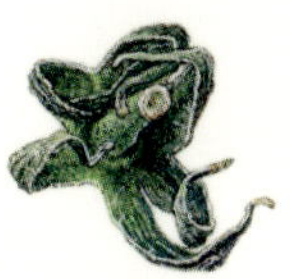

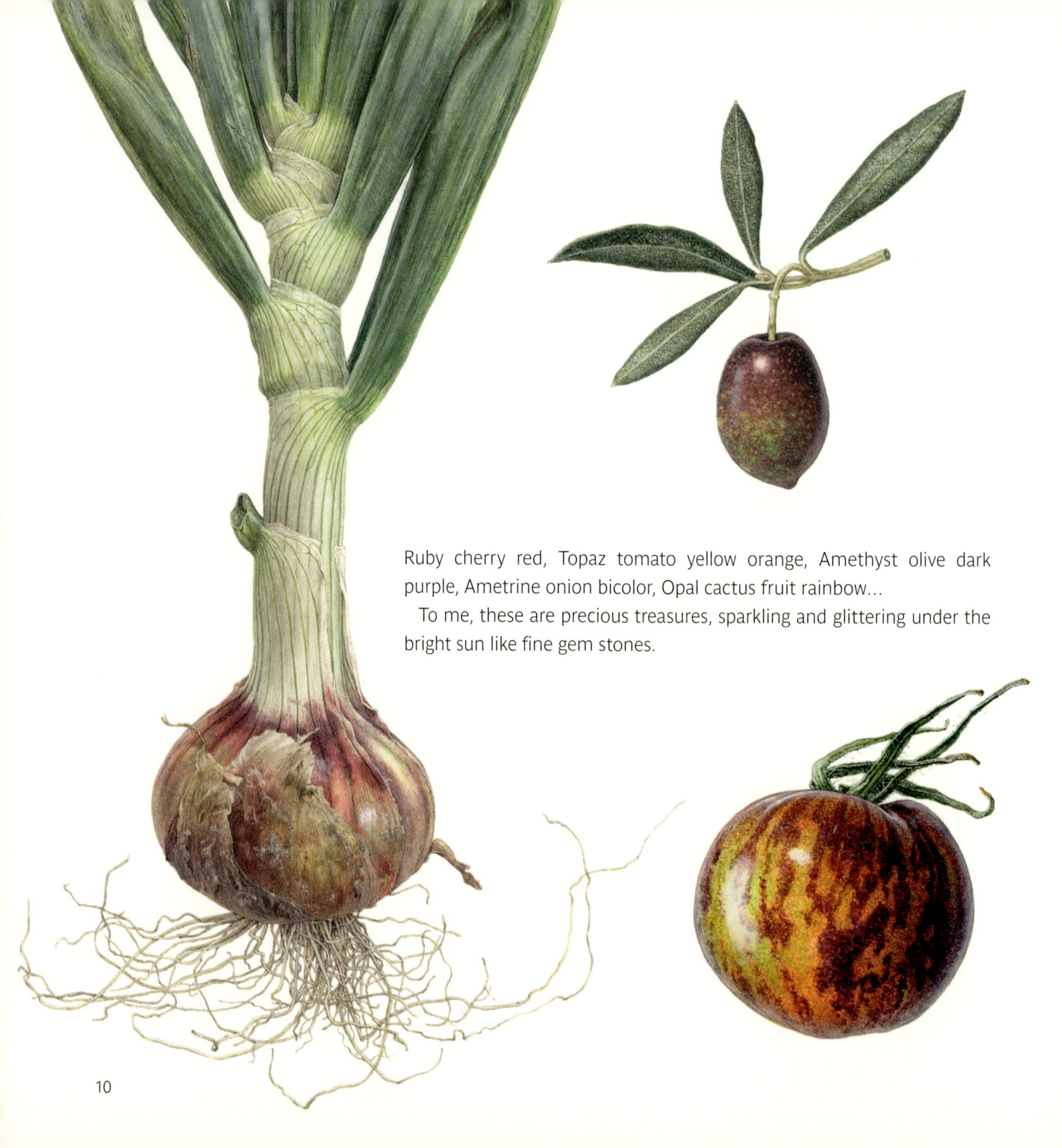

Ruby cherry red, Topaz tomato yellow orange, Amethyst olive dark purple, Ametrine onion bicolor, Opal cactus fruit rainbow…

To me, these are precious treasures, sparkling and glittering under the bright sun like fine gem stones.

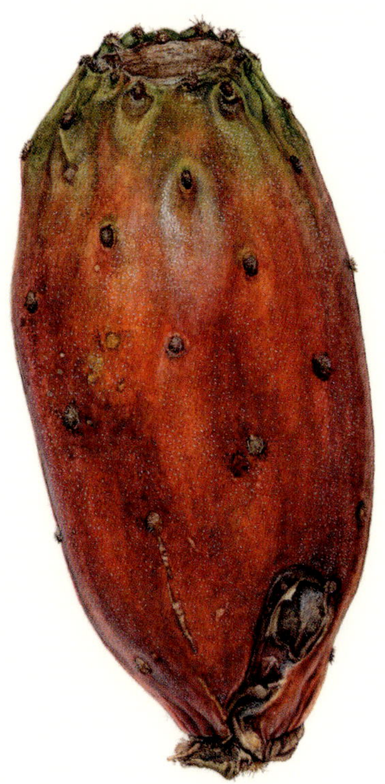

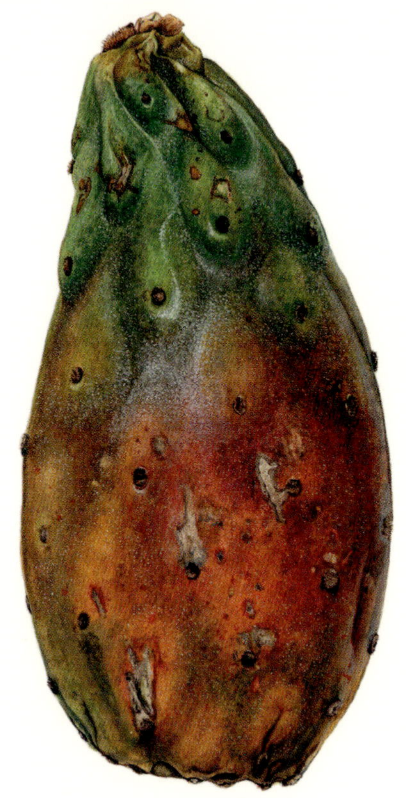

Rainbow Onion (2014)

Olive (2018)

Tiger jewel tomato (2021)

Cactus fruit (Prickly pear cactus, 2012)
Opuntia (unidentified species)

If you can change a pebble into pure gold, you will be rich beyond imagining. Unfortunately, I have no power to change anything into gold or gems, or anything valuable. Actually, come to think of it, I cannot change anything into anything. However much I try chanting or putting magic onto it, it won't be changed at all – although maybe I can bend it if it is soft or snap it into two if it is breakable.

However, I can turn a fresh fruit into a still, solid figure, a painting. And while my subject turns into a rotting, stinky mess, the stable image of the fruit is sitting gracefully on paper, unchanged and retaining all its glitter.

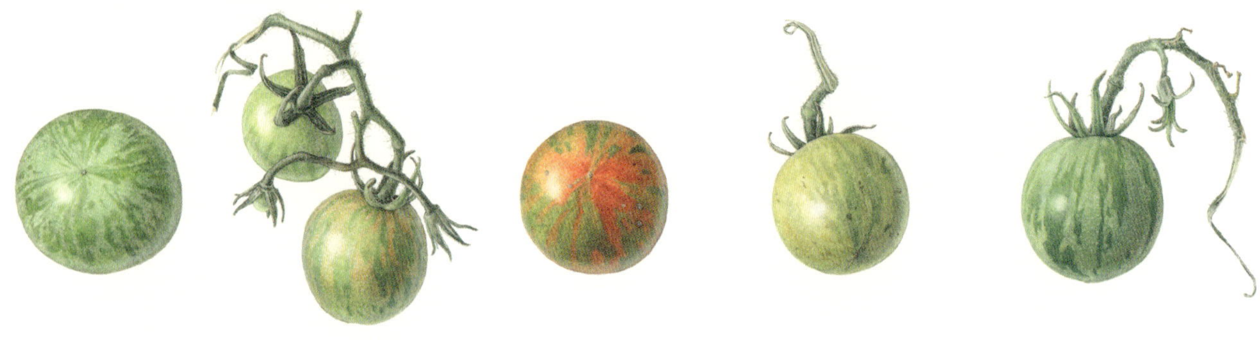

Children's Choir:
Four and a twin zebras (2015)

Have you ever watched a tomato turn from fresh green to mature red? Or any kind of fruit? Maybe not. It is normally already fully ripe when we see it on a supermarket shelf. Or maybe you see it changing colour if you grow it yourself. It will develop its colour slightly every day and it may be your daily routine to check the difference. However, it is rare to witness the colour actually turn, because it happens over a long period of time.

Most heirloom tomatoes remain green for a long time. Once ready, the colour turns very quickly. The pace is irregular and it all depends on temperature and sunlight and whether the fruits are still on the plant or cut from it. For several days, they stay a steady, pinky cream and pale green, then suddenly they start turning into seductive deep red. That may not be noticeable to you in only 10 minutes or so but working face to face with them for eight hours a day as I do, the change is obvious. But night-time makes me nervous, because sometimes I'll receive a surprise next morning, for the tomatoes can change dramatically overnight. I repeatedly ask them to stay the same, as I wish to catch their best colour. But there is nothing I can do. Time passes and the colour keeps changing.

**A portrait of a heirloom tomato:
Dancing duo (2015)**

It's an amazing thing working with nature. Even if I miss the best colour, the change may bring something even better. I cannot stop the tomatoes fading or decaying, but it means I don't miss their peak. And who knows, the next stage may be the better one.

The colour peak is not, however, the taste peak. My subjects are often not safe to eat fresh once I've finished painting them, so soups and jams are a typical solution. By then, they're over-ripe so the soups and jams usually taste particularly nice (but not always).

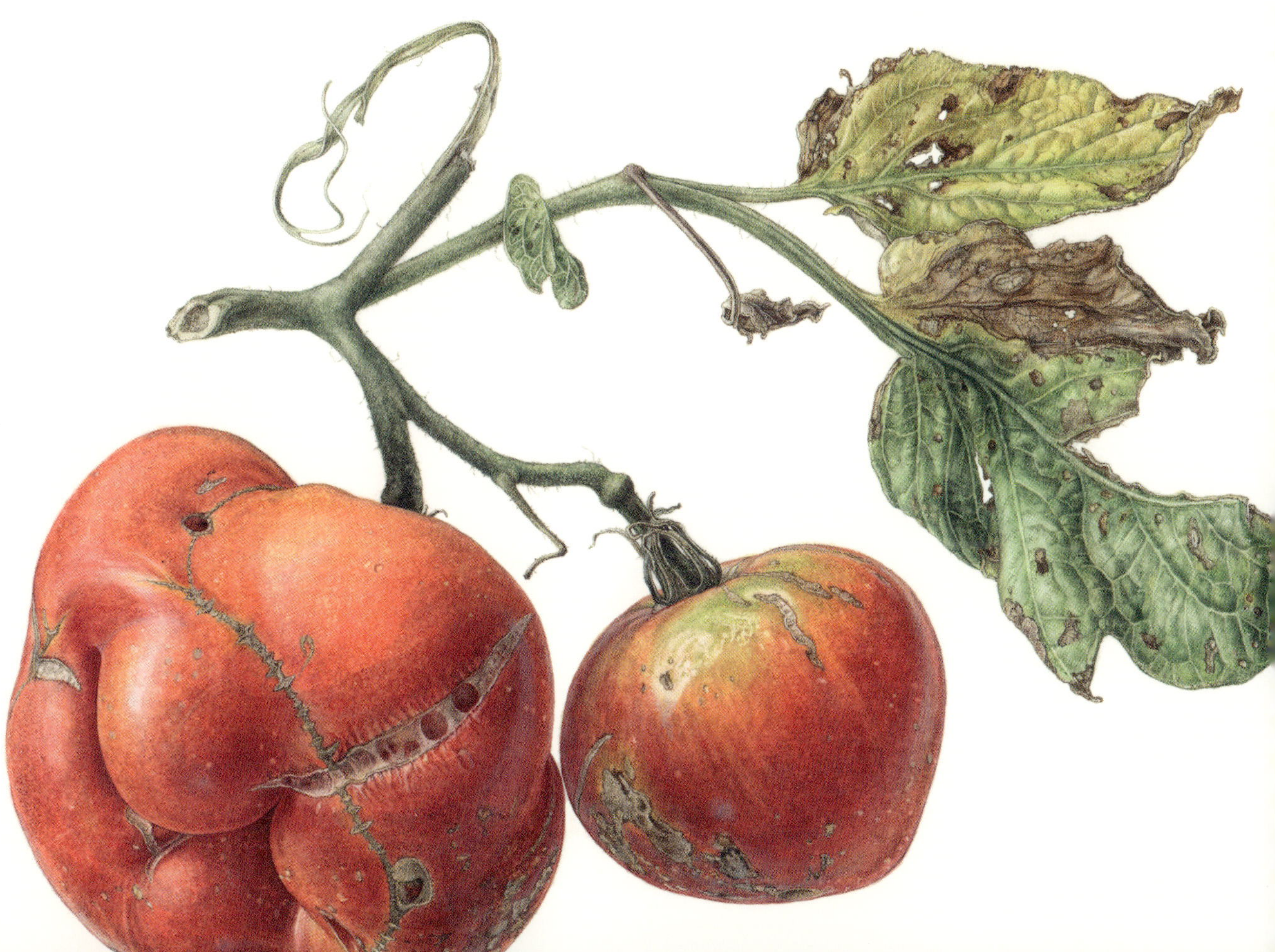

Turezure no kusa:
Pomegranate (2021)

Turezure no kusa:
Pomegranates on a tree (2022)

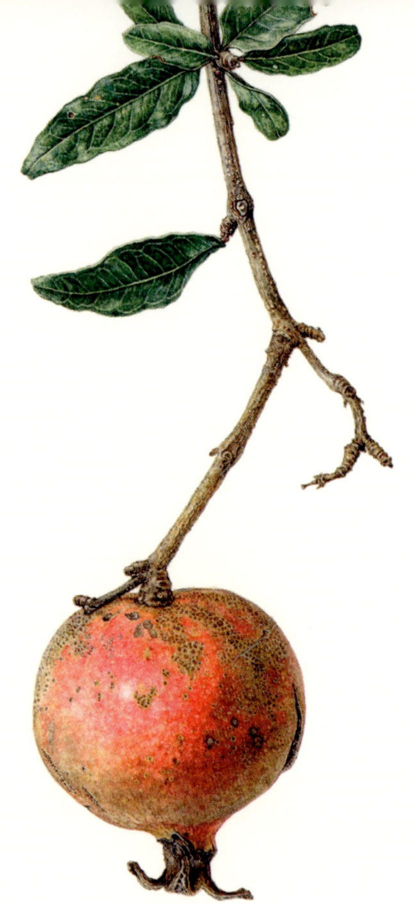

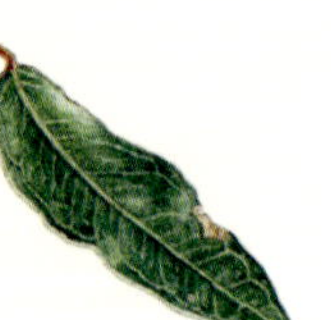

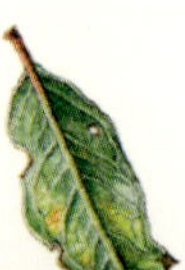

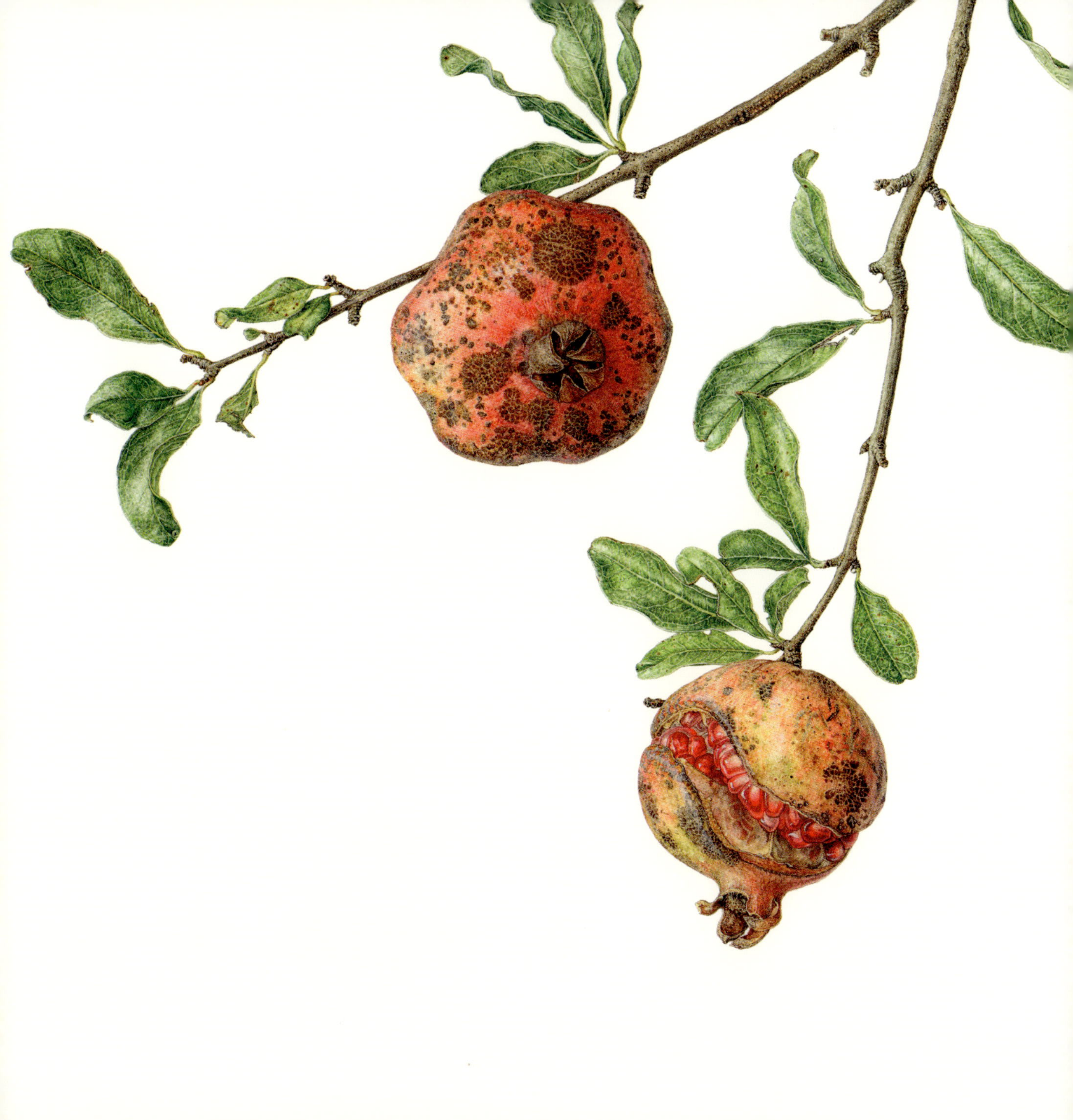

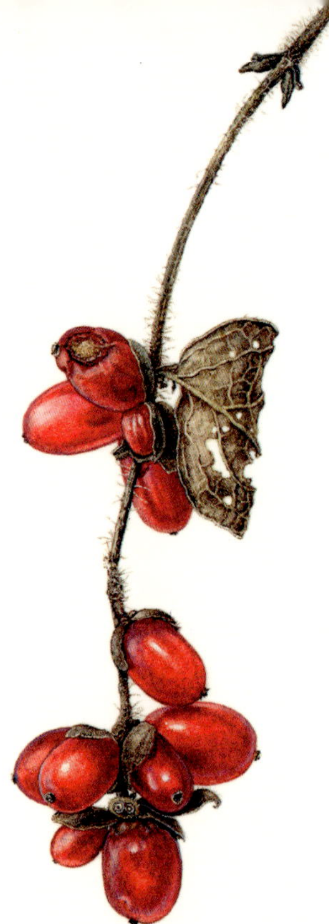

Lonicera cerasina Maxim is an endangered species around my area and its charming, shiny, red fruits are toxic. Although you may not be in serious danger, you will be sick for sure if you eat them. We tend to think that 'natural products' are tender and good for our health, but in this case, the vivid red is a warning. So pay attention, do not eat!

However, the colour of cherry red is very inviting and tempts you to take a bite. Every spring, my eyes are on the wild cherry tree in our backyard as I check the best moment to pick them. The peak season is very short.

The fully ripe cherries and the toxic fruits look very similar in colour, but beware, because one gives a warning, the other an invitation.

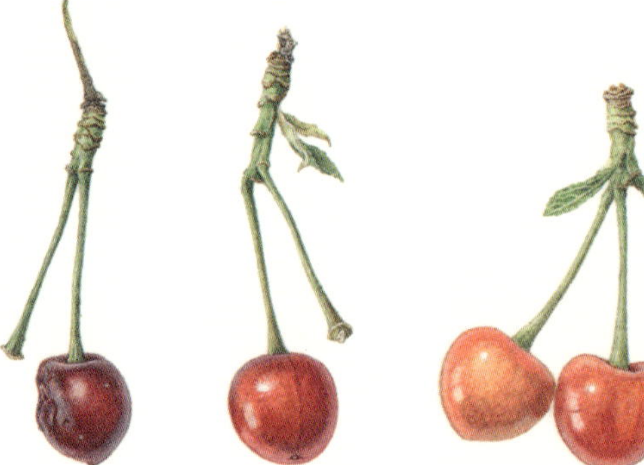

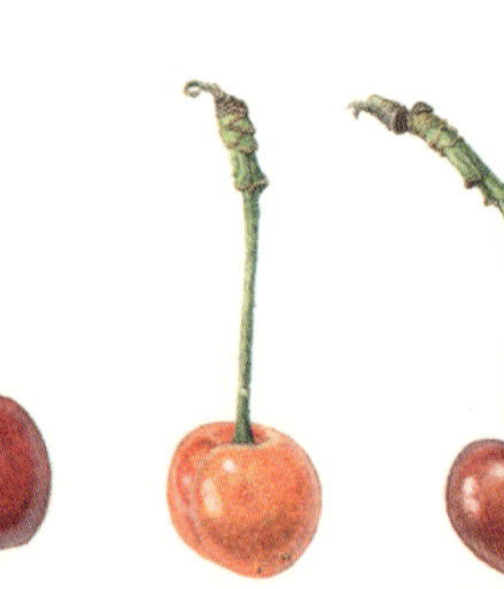

Turezure no kusa:
Red poisonous fruits (2018)

Wild cherry (2018)

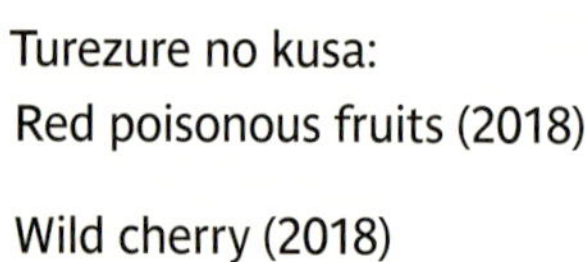

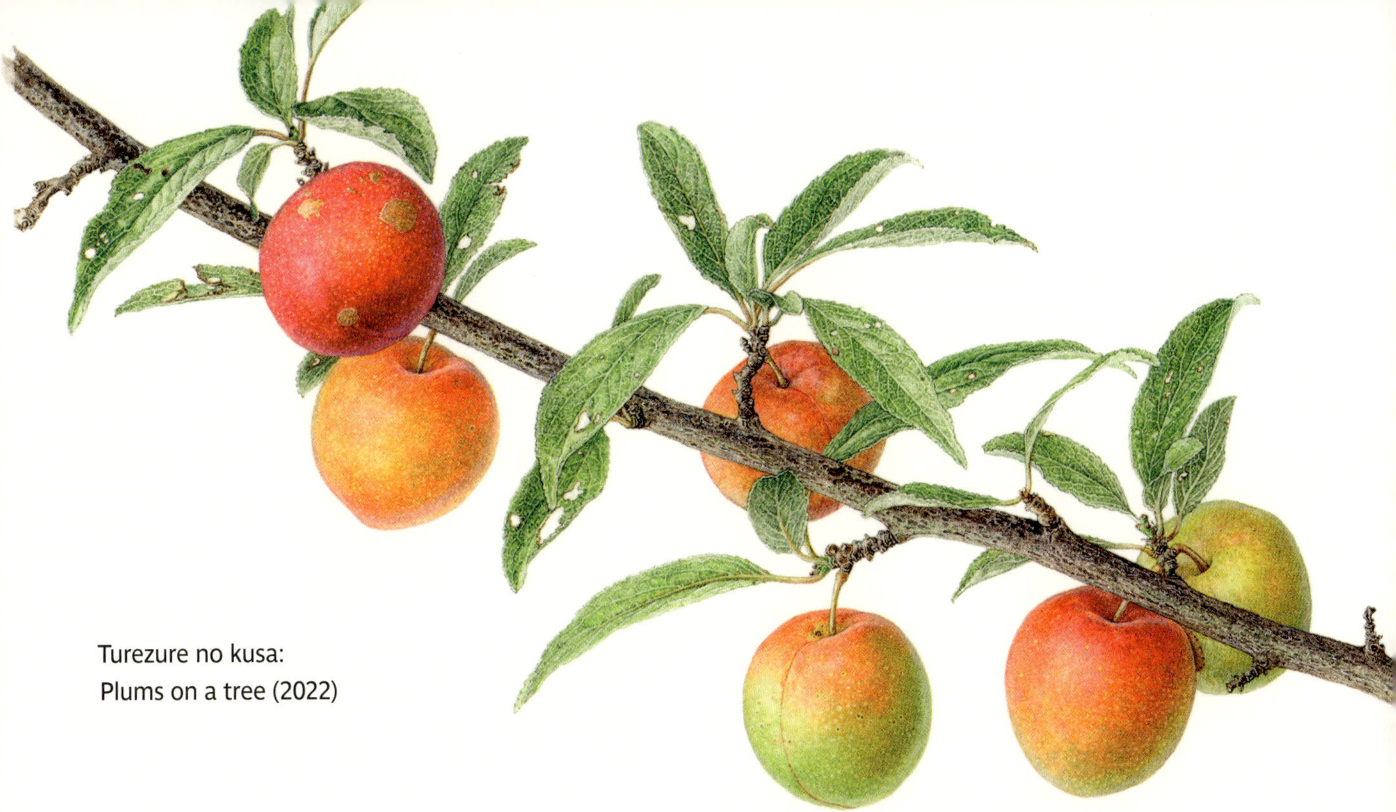

Turezure no kusa:
Plums on a tree (2022)

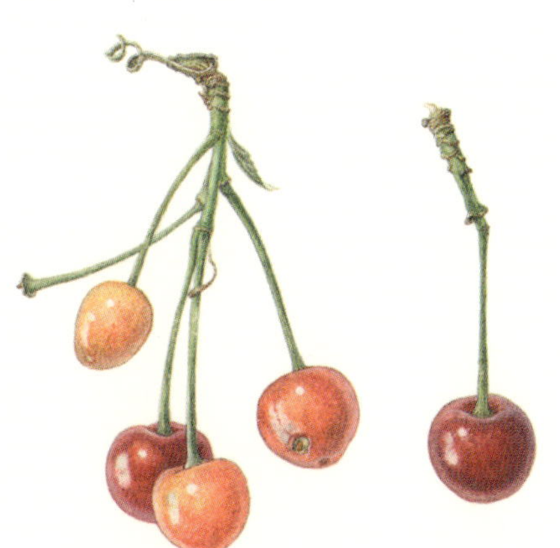

These plums were given to me by a relative who farms as a hobby. They were not sweet but sour, yet sour in a pleasant way. The plum tree was grown from the pit of a fruit she ate in the field. Look at the variation of colour. The tree grew and grew, so the soil of her farm must be really good. This spring, the tree brought her two baskets full of plums.

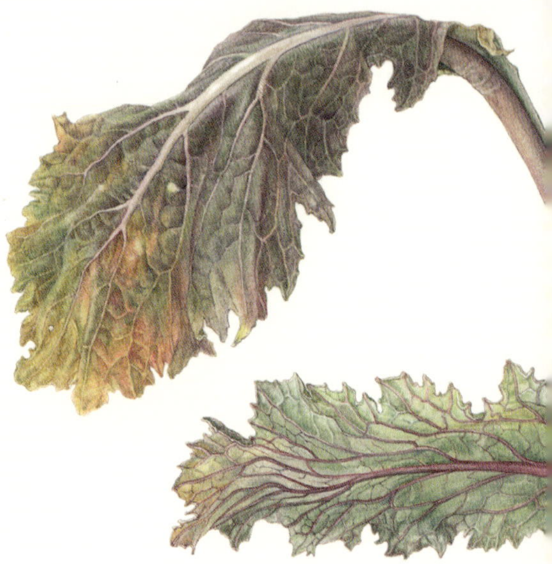

Turnip (Ayameyuki, 2015)
Brassica rapa var. *rapa*

Mundane, daily vegetables. But something about them is very handsome.

However much I try, I can never satisfactorily explain how beautiful they are. Actually, I am often disappointed that we have just the word 'beautiful' to describe them. There are many kinds of beauty in a subject, yet my poor language can't manage to describe them.

Rainbow sparkles on the leaves, moon crater-like scars on the purple and snow-white skin… Very romantic and very dramatic. I'm hoping that my work does a better job of saying much, much more than my words.

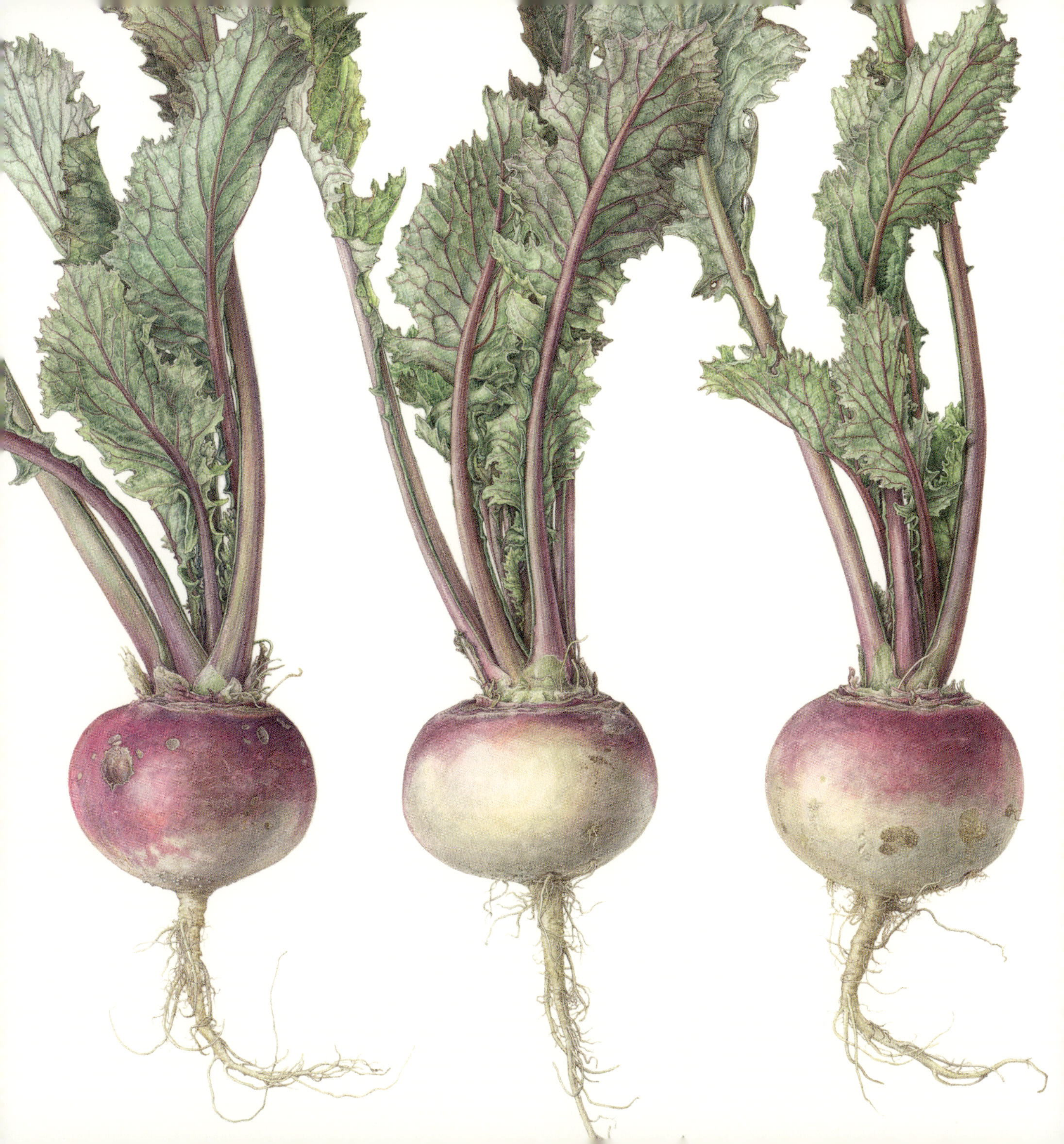

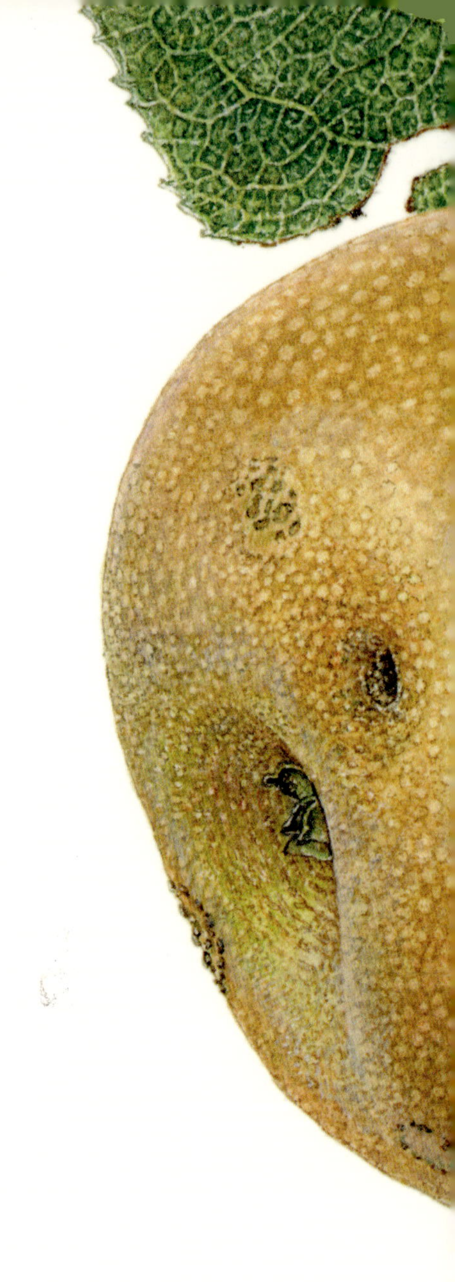

Turezure no kusa
Pears on a tree (2022)

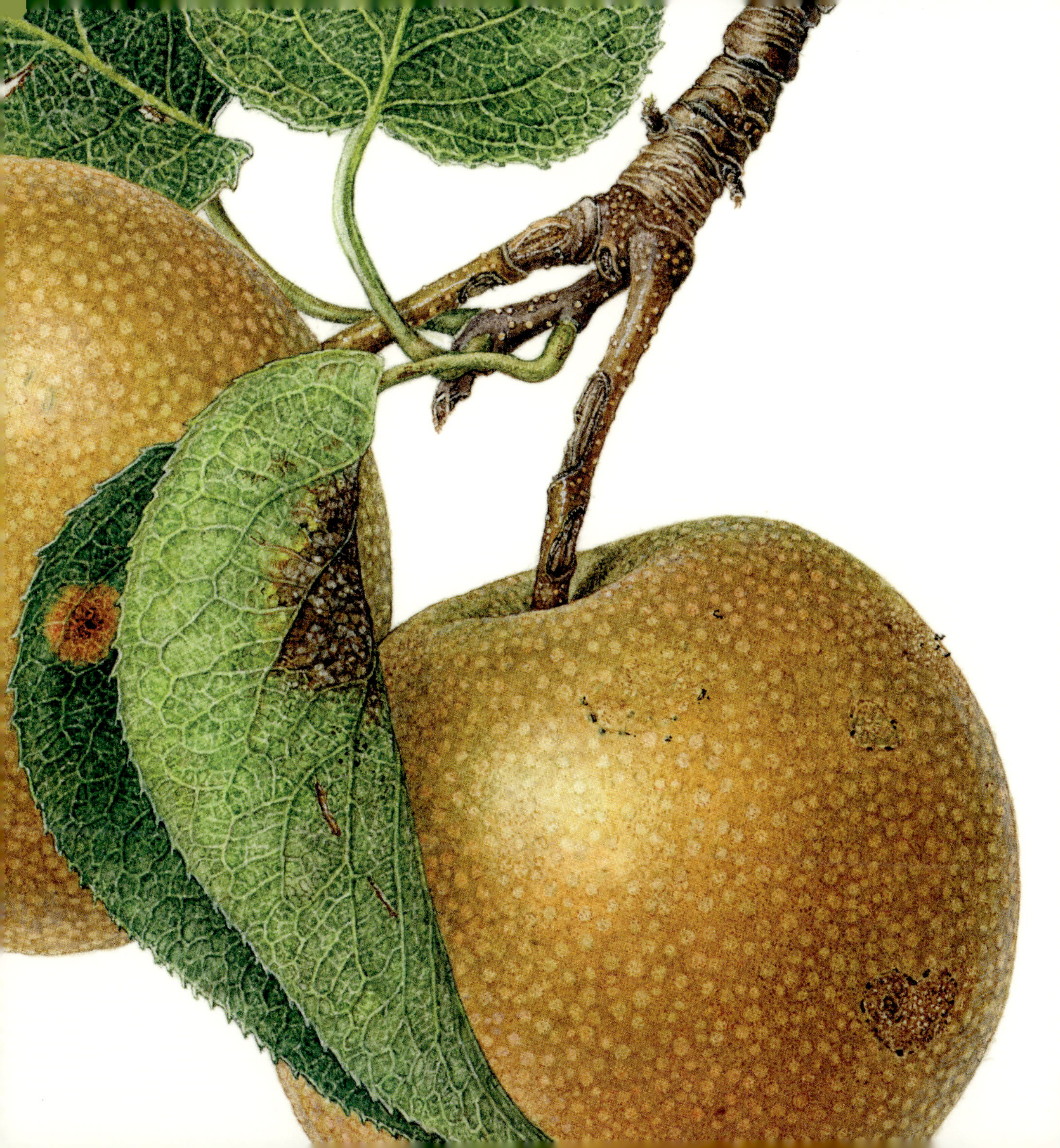

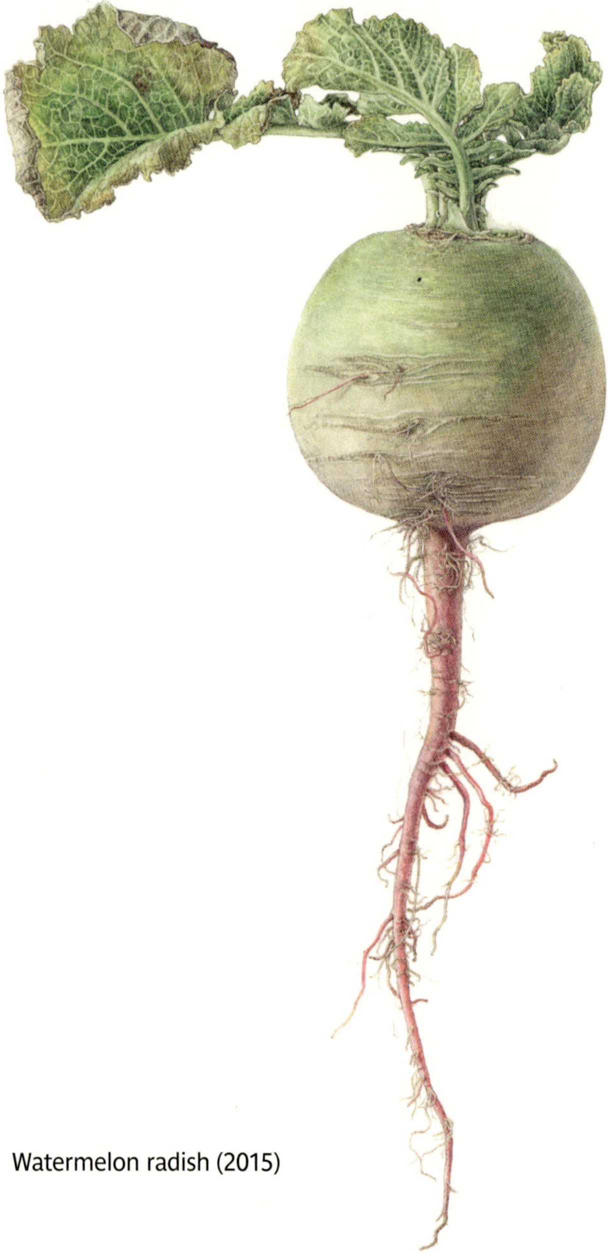

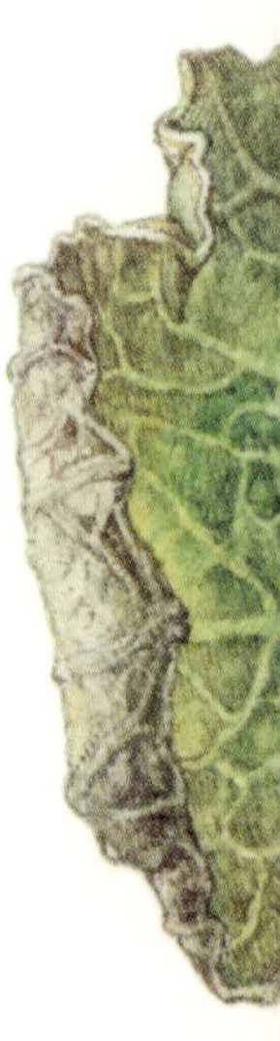

Watermelon radish (2015)

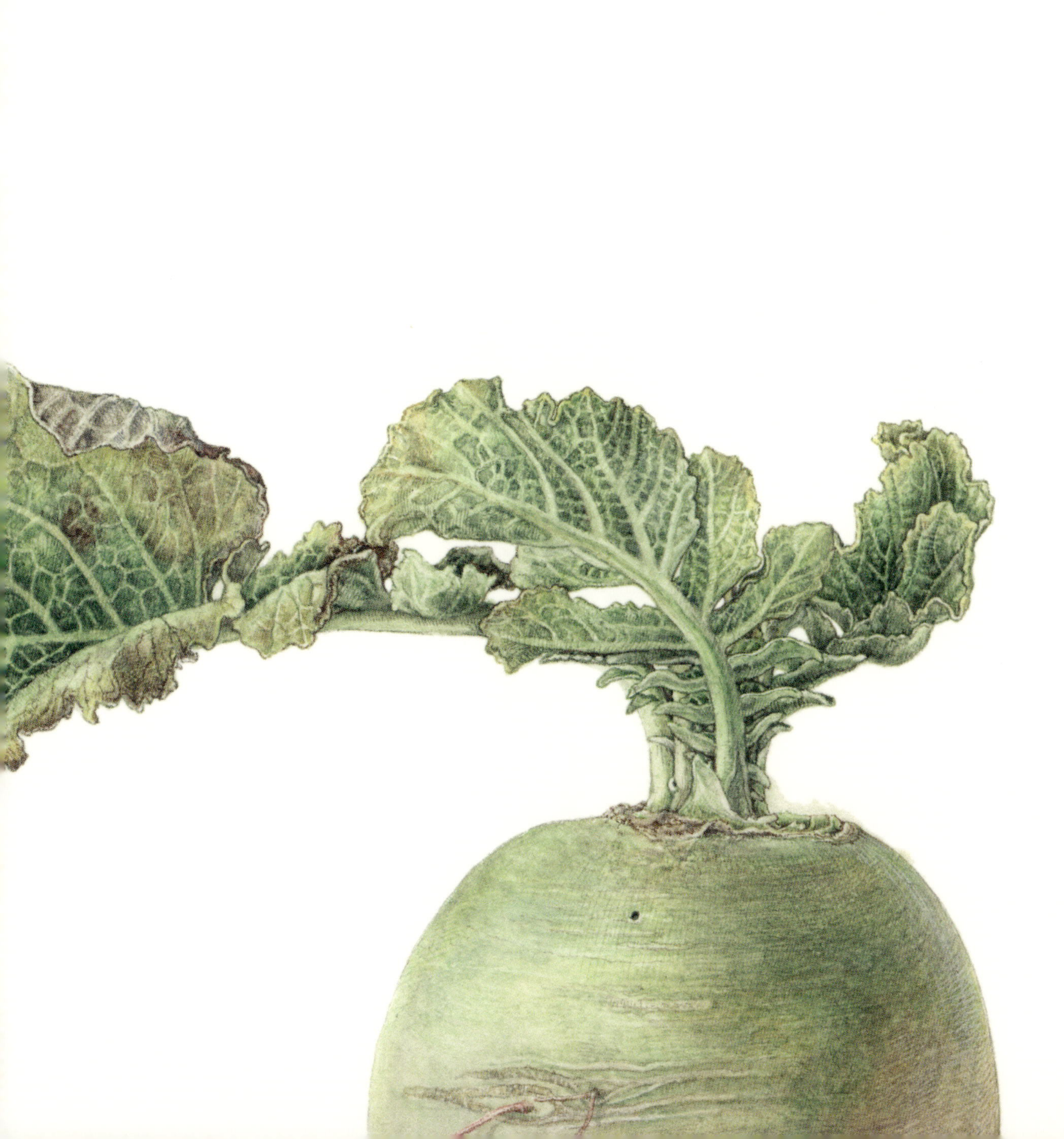

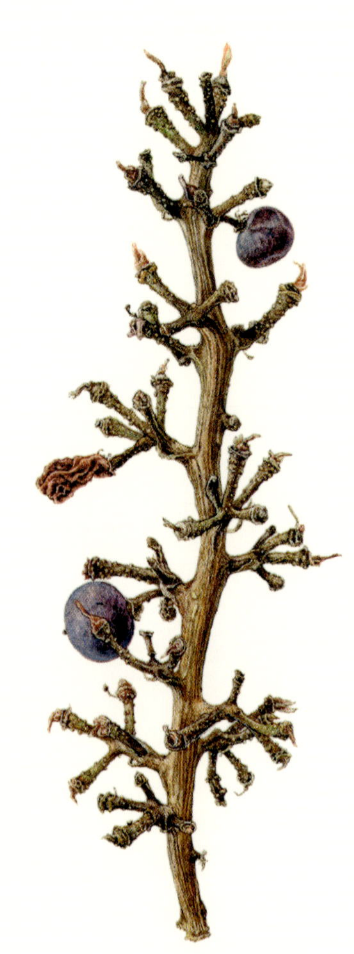

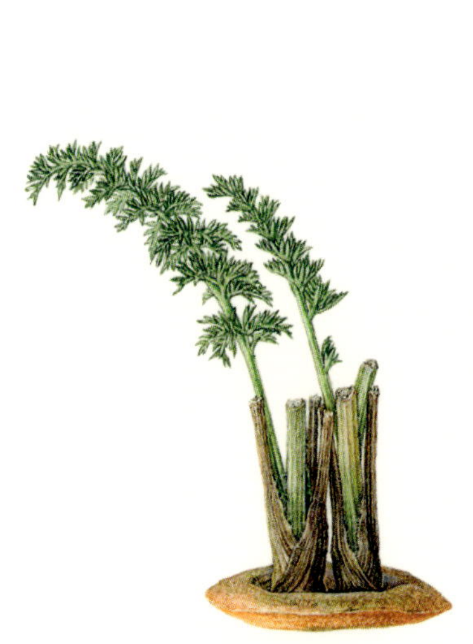
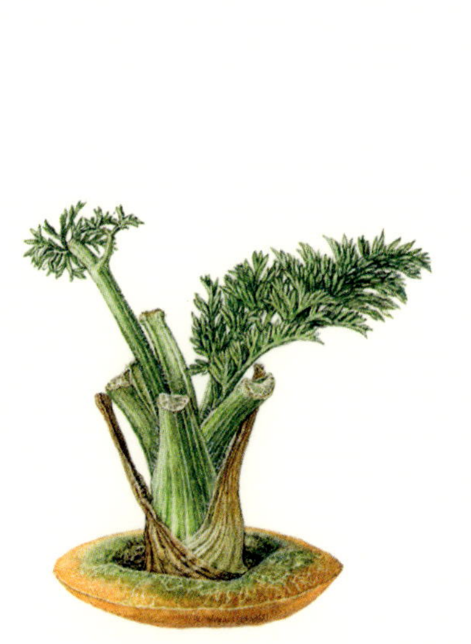
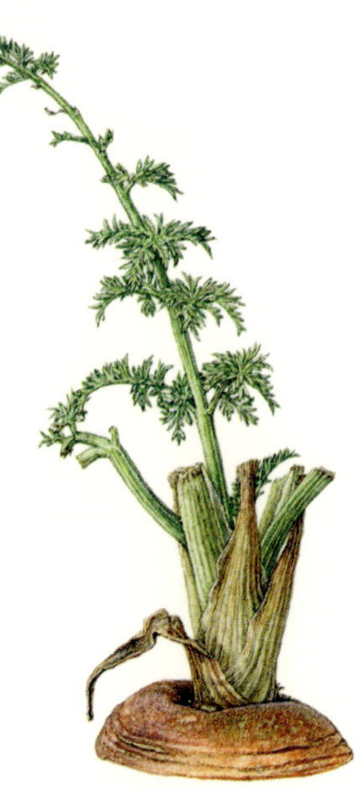

Turezure no kusa:
Grape stem (2018)

Turezure no kusa:
Three carrot tops (2018)

I have a really bad habit. I cannot resist saving odd bits of kitchen trash if they look great: offcuts and peelings like vegetable skins, fruit pits, woody stalks, stems and nut shells. I know it probably won't be useful– you cannot eat it and it won't be any good for decoration. It will soon be dry, rotten or mouldy, ending up as rubbish in my compost. But that good-looking rubbish is still attractive to me.

Grape stems are a bit like winter street trees in my neighbourhood. And to me, carrot tops are like mini bonsai.

But my 'saves' are not all useless. You can save a top from a root vegetable and grow a bit of green from it. I use the green as decoration on our dinner plates, and on top of pasta or soup it looks great. And, of course, they can sit to pose for me as well.

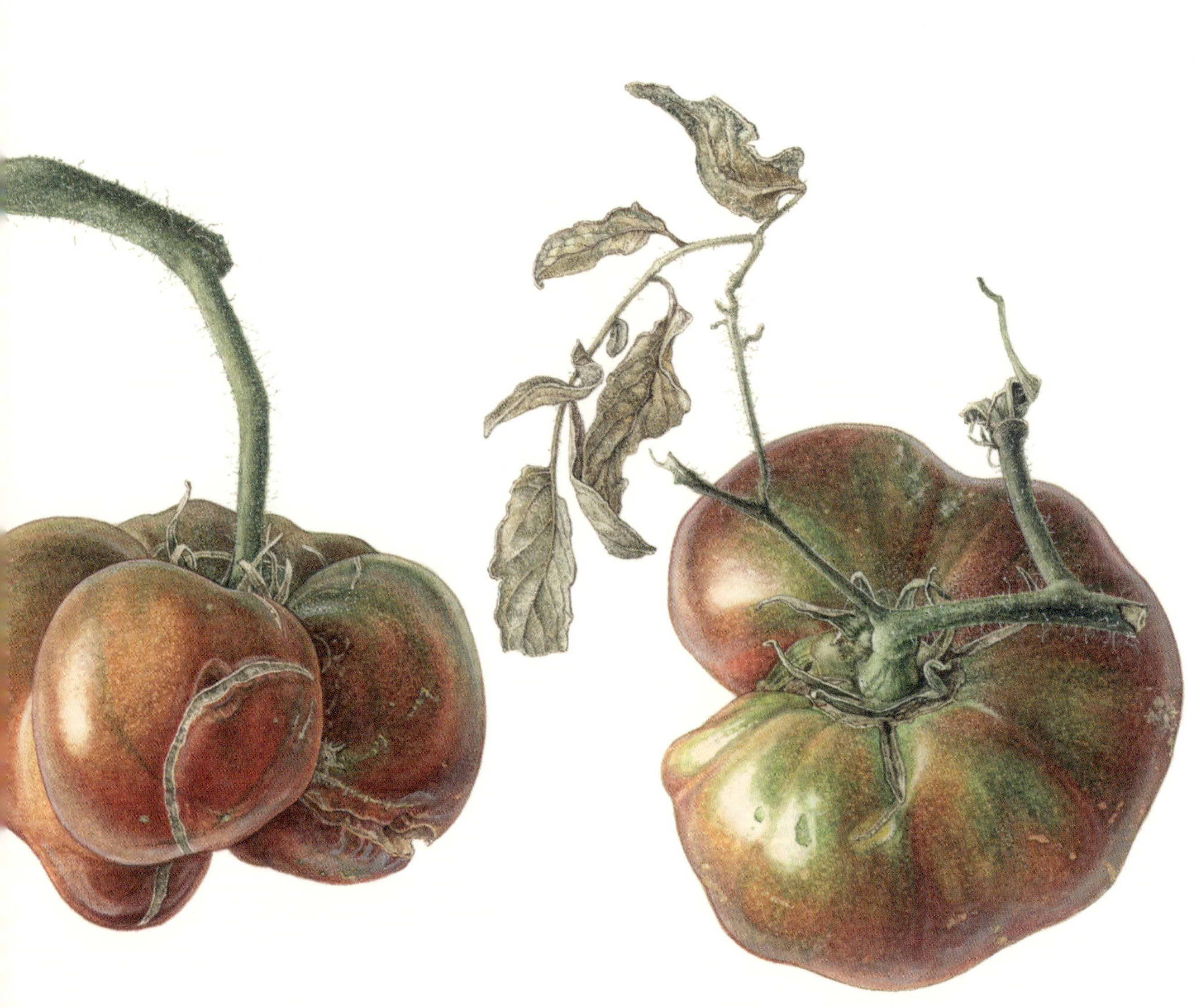

II. Messy business

Badly scarred, desperately tangled, and horribly bushy

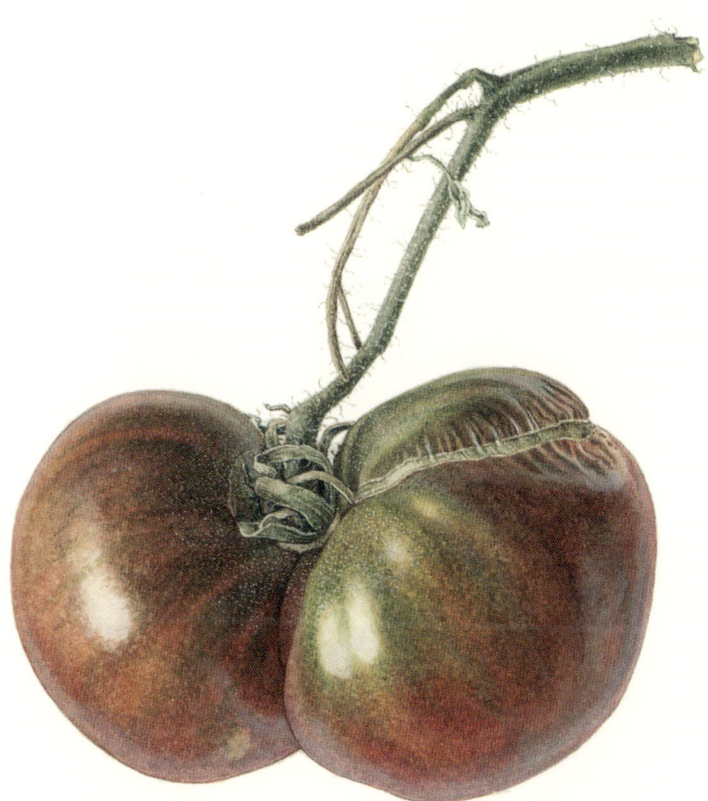

A portrait of a heirloom tomato:
Brandies (2016)

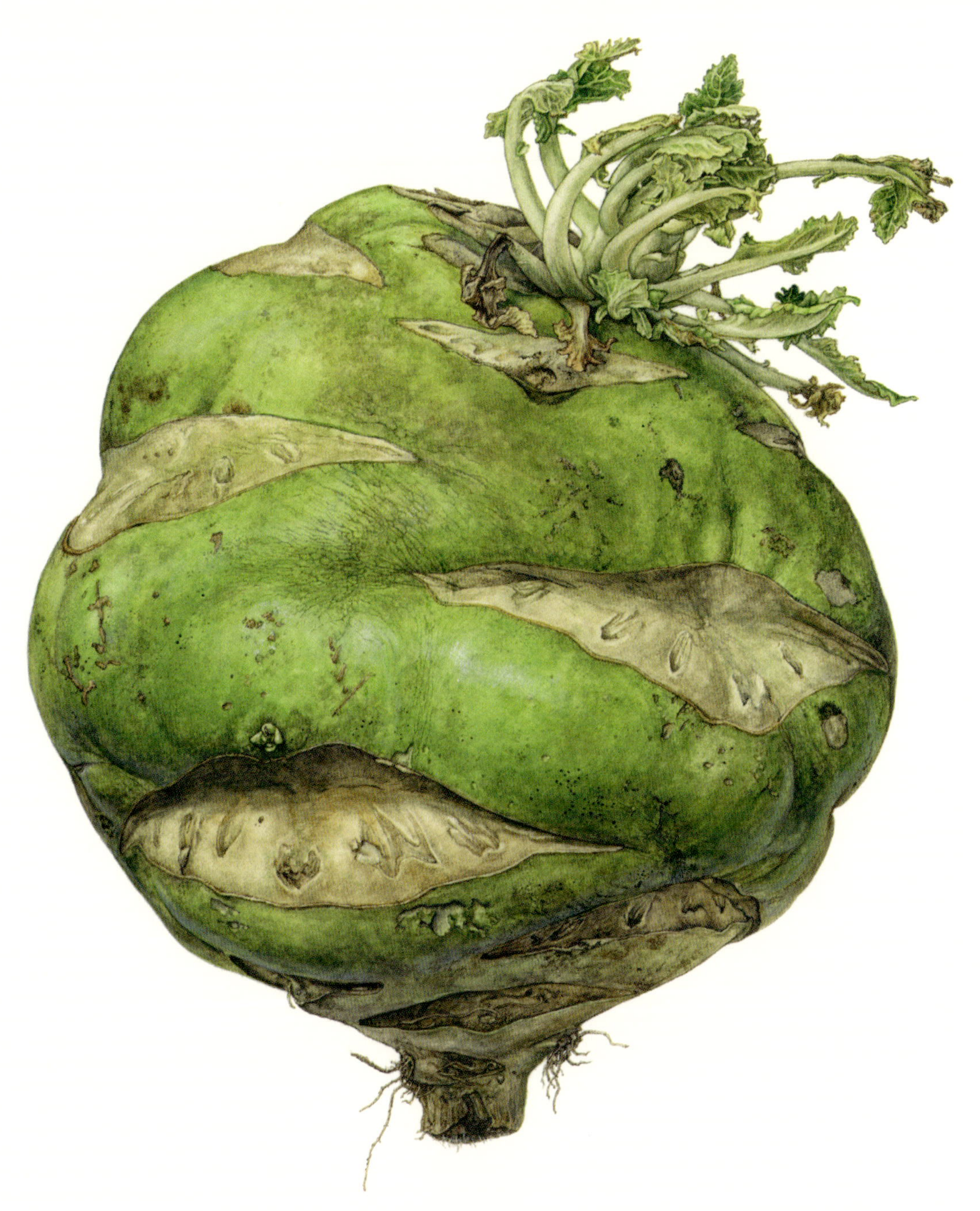

Not because I like to torture myself, but somehow I am attracted to rather complicated and tormented-looking subjects – they are proof that they fought to be alive. Even badly scarred, they grow into big roots or fruits. Bushy roots and leaves are remarkable evidence that plants have flourished well during their life. Like a veteran pirate, scars on vegetables are a badge of pride indicating bravery or strength. Well, actually, they may not be so to farmers, as the scarred or misshapen vegetables have very low commercial value. Yet I find them intriguing, and these one-of-a-kind features are simply attractive.

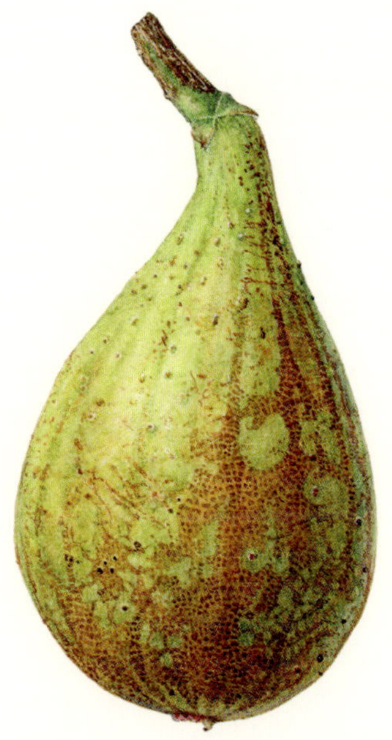

Giant kohlrabi (German turnip, 2012)
Brassica oleracea

Fig (2020)
Ficus carica

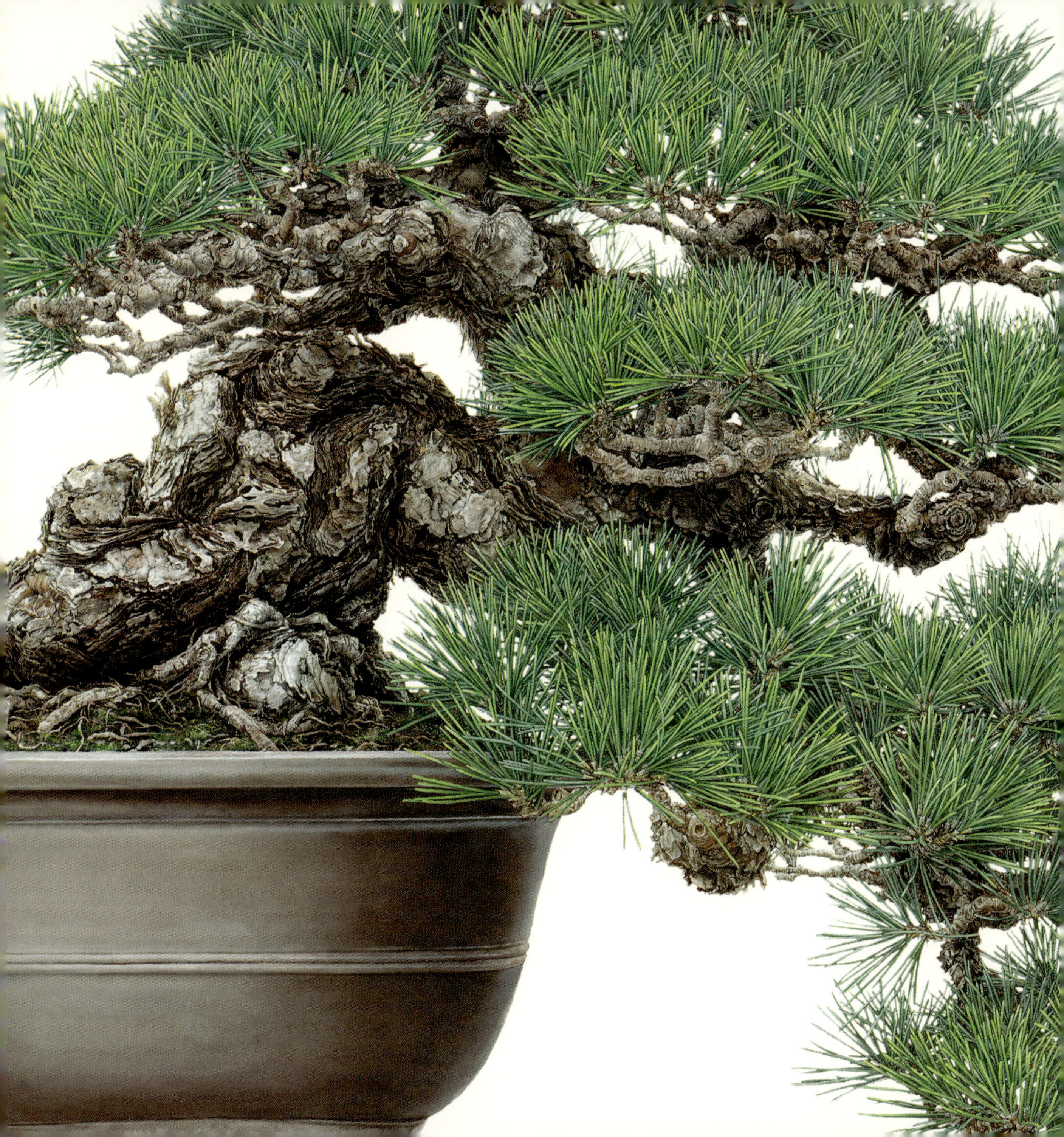

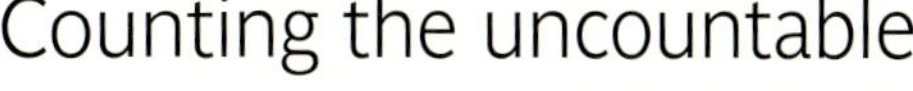

Counting the uncountable

Black Pine Half-cascade-style Bonsai (2015–2017)
Pinus nigra

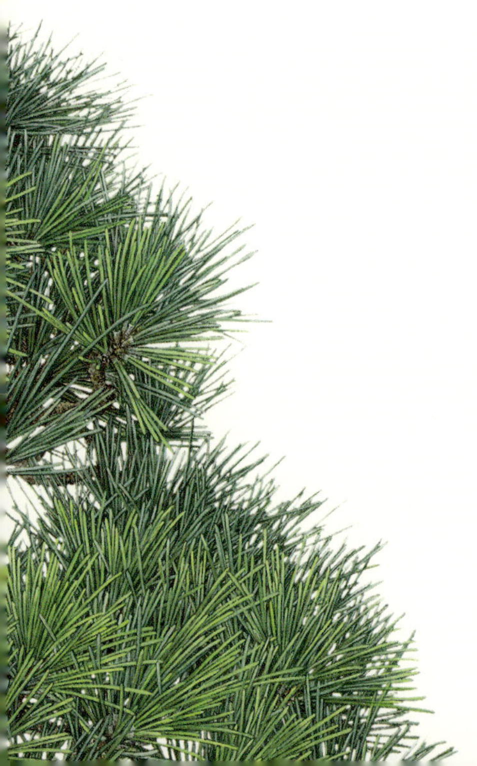

A cherry blossom has five petals and a peach has one pit (seed) inside each fruit. However, it is almost impossible to know how many leaves, or needles, a huge bonsai tree has. So, to paint it faithfully, all I can do is follow the structural logic. Black pine needles are about 7–12 cm long and two needles are bundled together (as a fascicle) at the base with a white sheath. Just observe really well the structure of the tree and see where the twin needles are coming from, which direction they point in, which branch is located in front and which at the back and so on. It is a nightmarish practice. The painting emerges slowly, very slowly – one pair of needles after another.

The tree is about 250 years old and I wonder if it met Hokusai? Nightmare or daydream, either way, I must be in a trance, counting the uncountable…

Fern (2013)

Dryopteris erythrosora

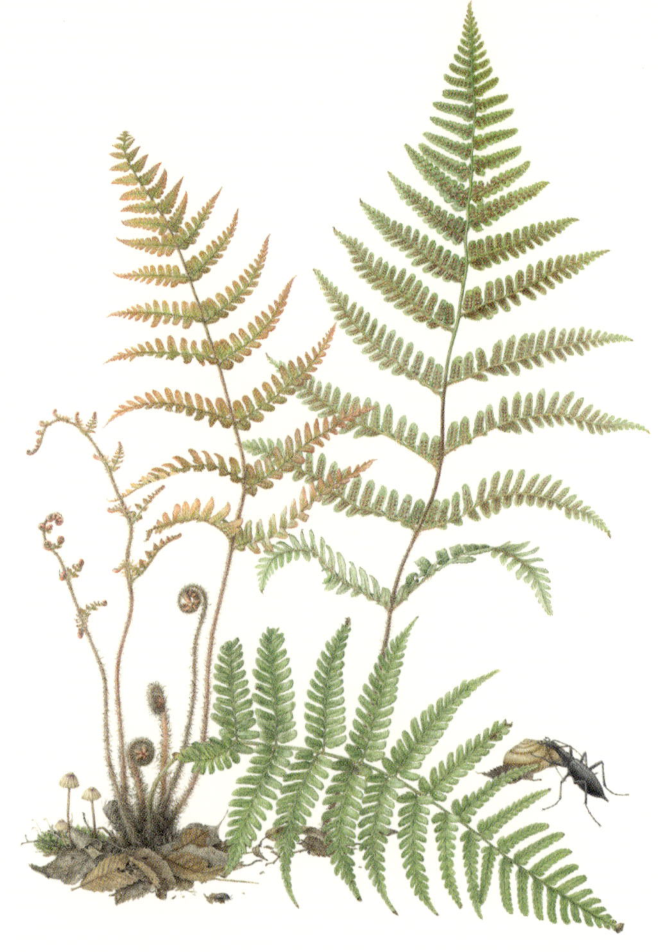

The fern sori are countable, but all are following strict 'fern rules'. So I counted all the sori (brown spots containing spores) on each section of the leaf (pinna). The under-drawing is full of numbers indicating how many of them were on each section, and I tried to keep track of which one I was painting. It was difficult not to mix it up with the one next to it though–they all look alike!

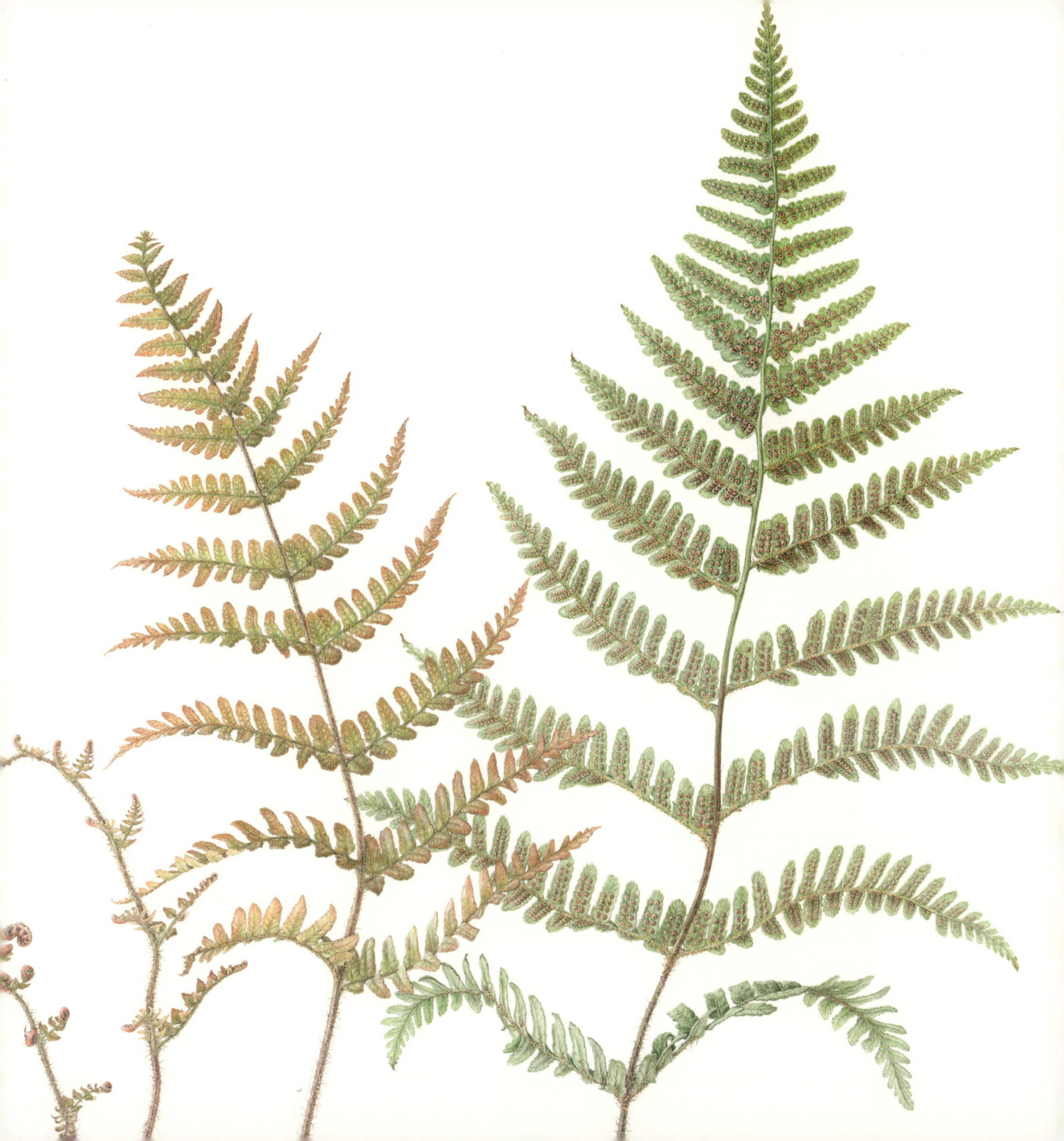

On the other hand, wasabi root is simply a mess and there is no structural logic nor countable features. In fact, looking back, I do not remember how I managed to capture the whole root.

In each case, I was strongly tempted to mark where I was painting directly onto the subject, but there was no way I could make a physical mark on them. Pins or tapes were too heavy, and paints or marker pen disturbed the colour balance. This is how the negotiation goes between me and the subject.

I know I am the one who picks a subject every time, but often I get lost in a painting and start mumbling grudgingly at myself. 'Why did I pick this?', I ask.

The breadfruit is a classic jigsaw puzzle. If I miss a piece, it will ruin the whole sequence. It's a good thing it is heavy and big, so I can mark several of the characteristic disks on the fruit with my kneaded eraser and count off from there – one, two, three from the mark… four, five, six…

But my gosh, why did I pick this?

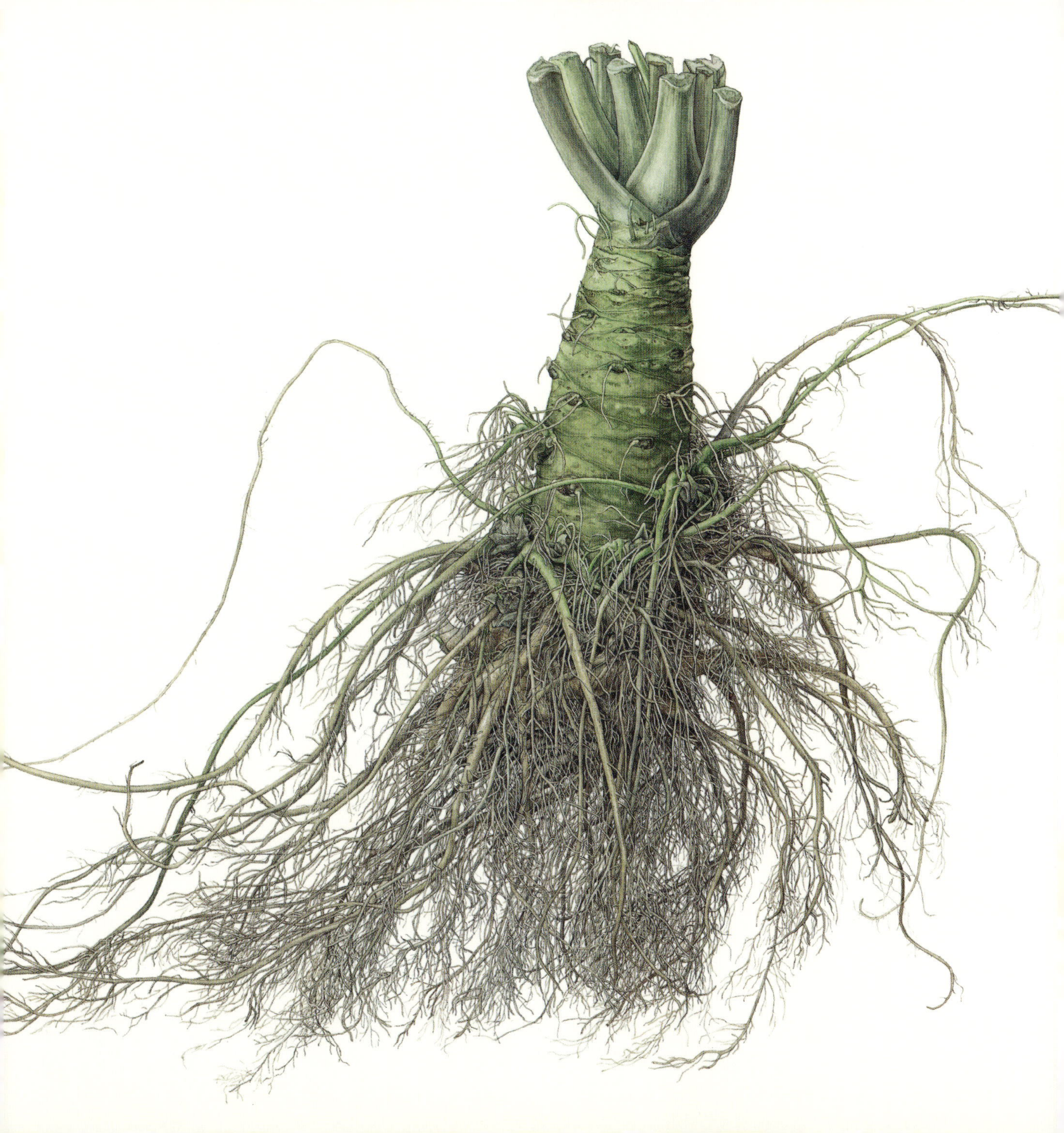

Broccoli (2014)
Brassica oleracea

Black walnut (2011)
Juglans nigra

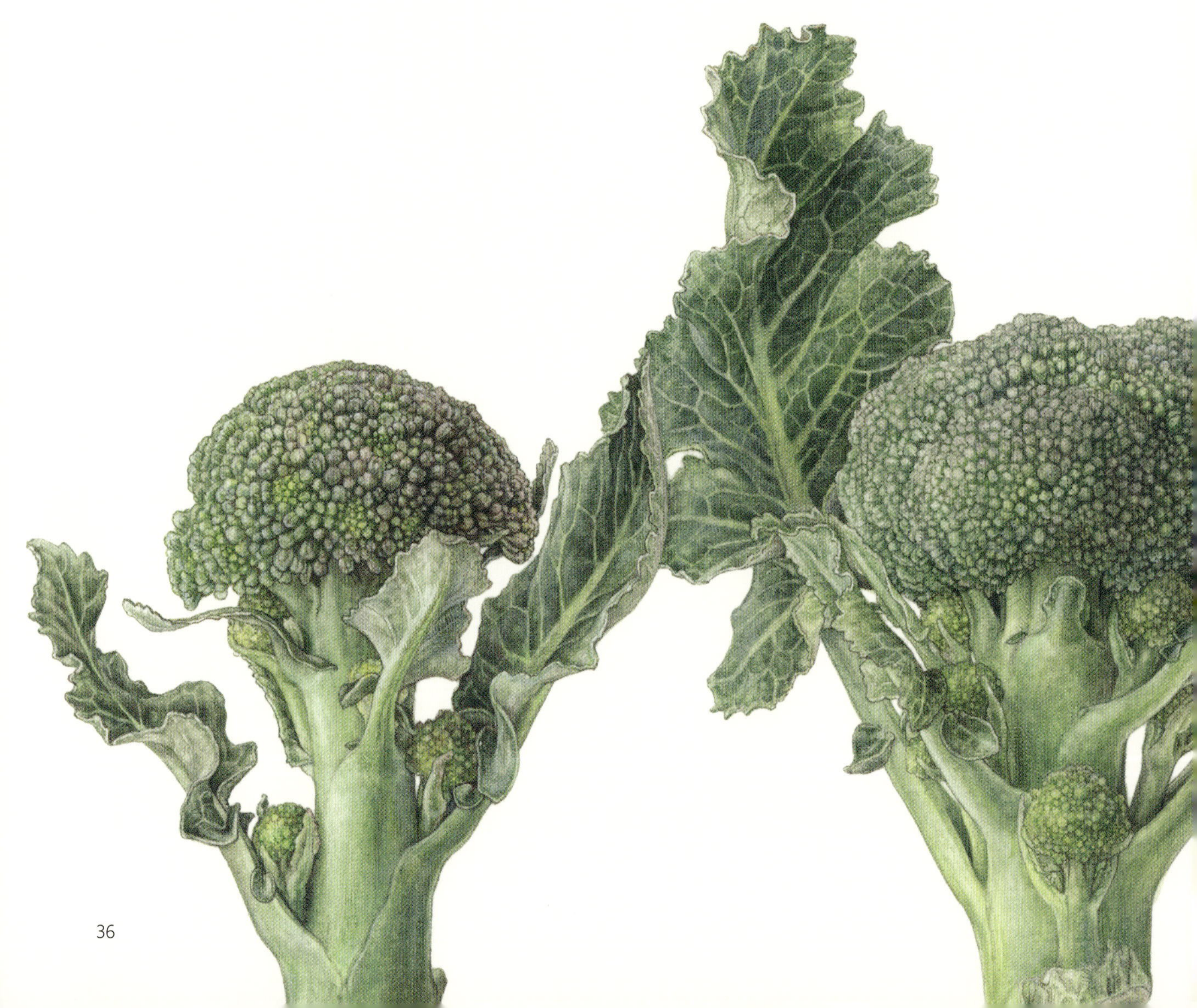

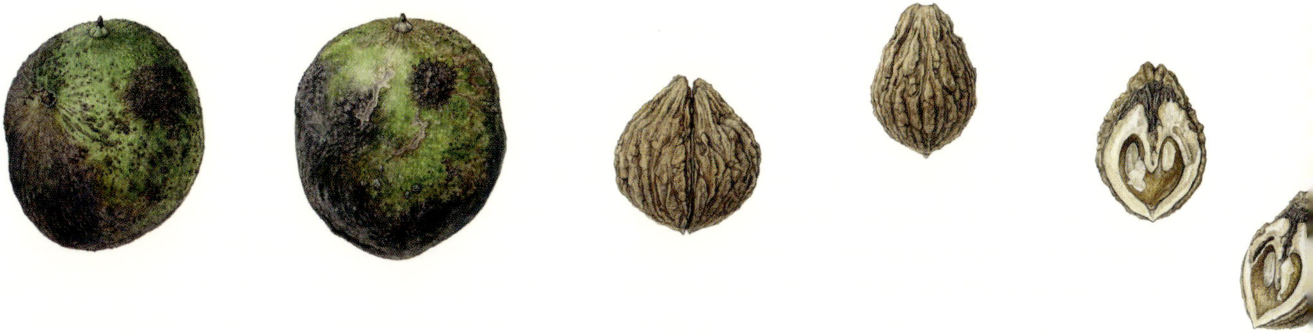

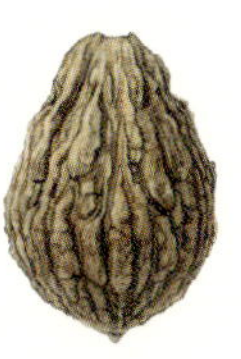
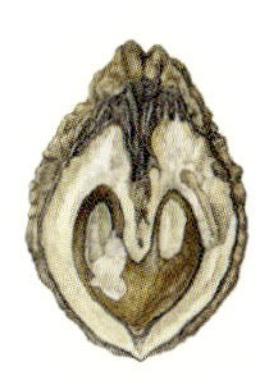
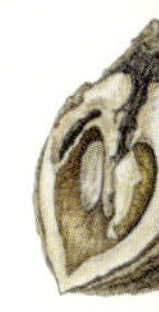

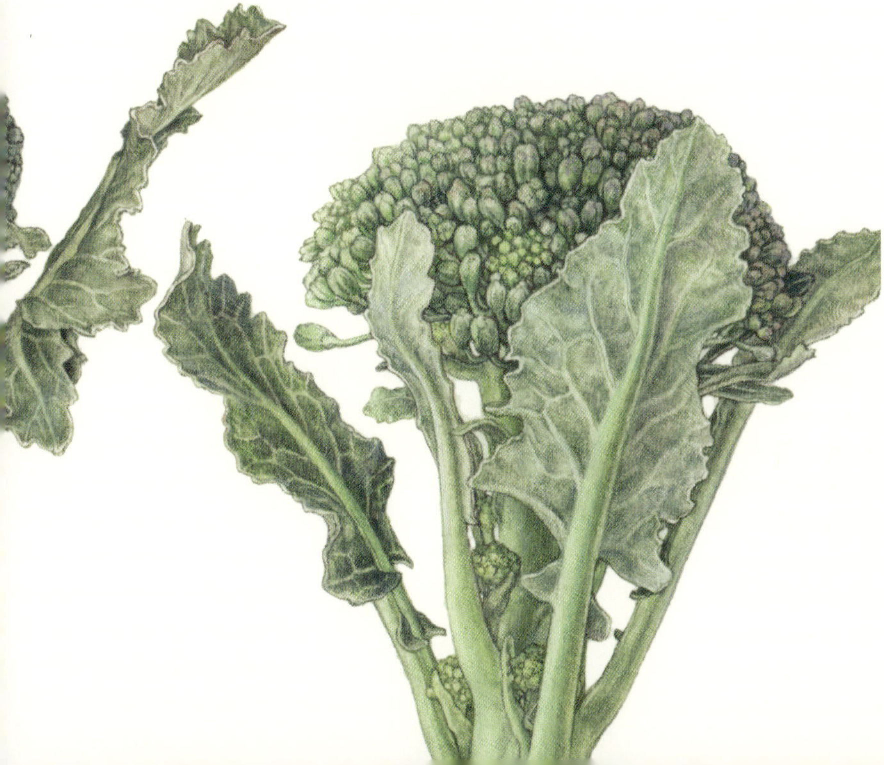

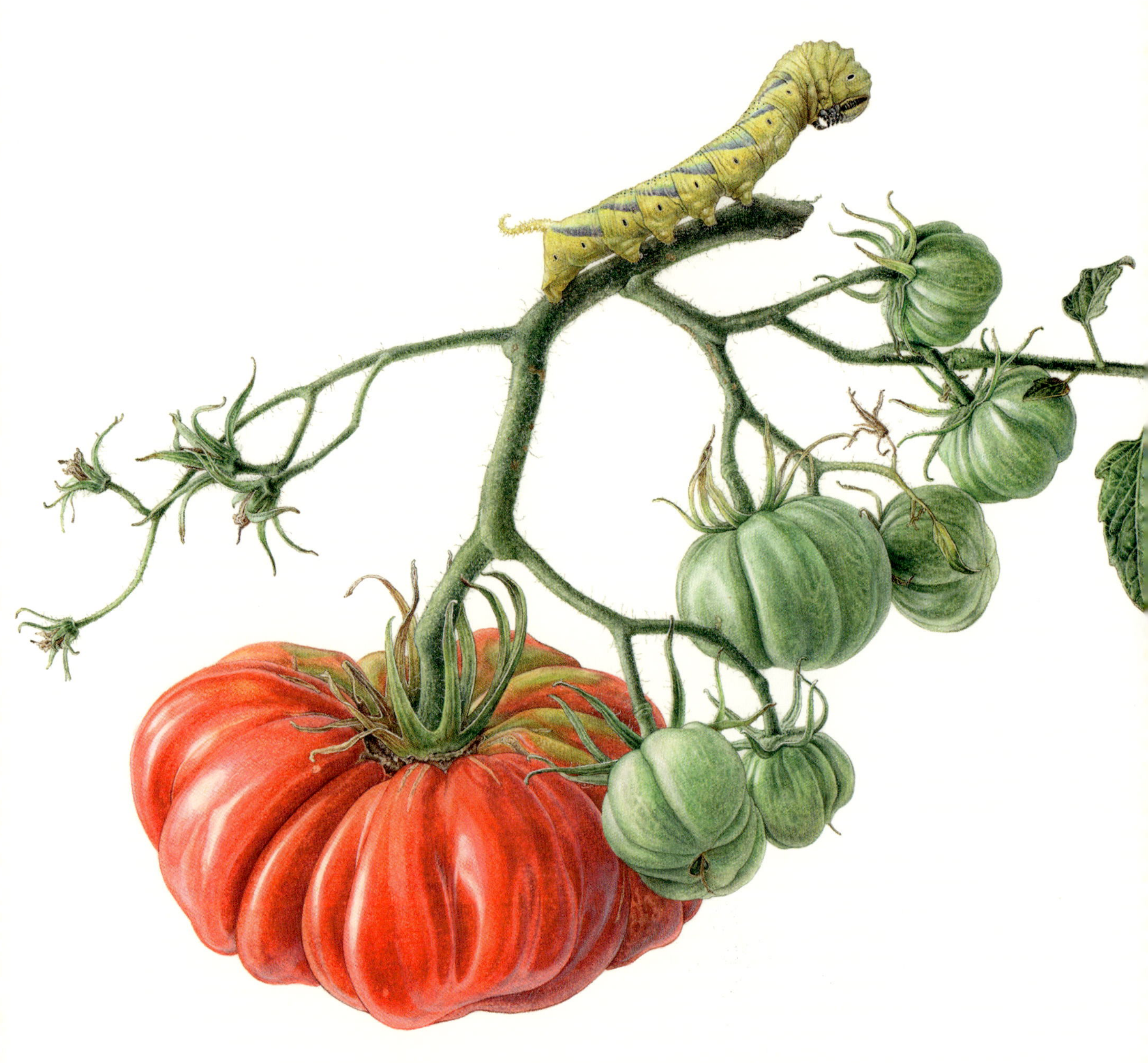

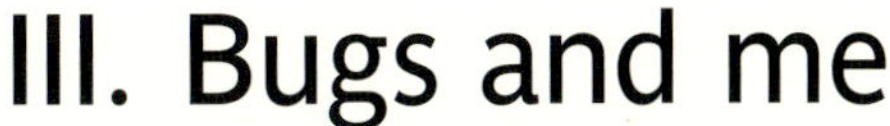

III. Bugs and me

A love-hate relationship

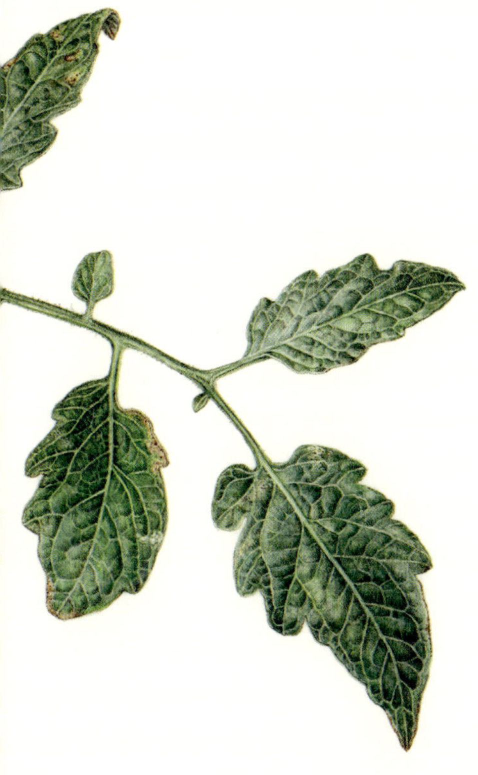

A portrait of a heirloom tomato:
Pirates (2016)

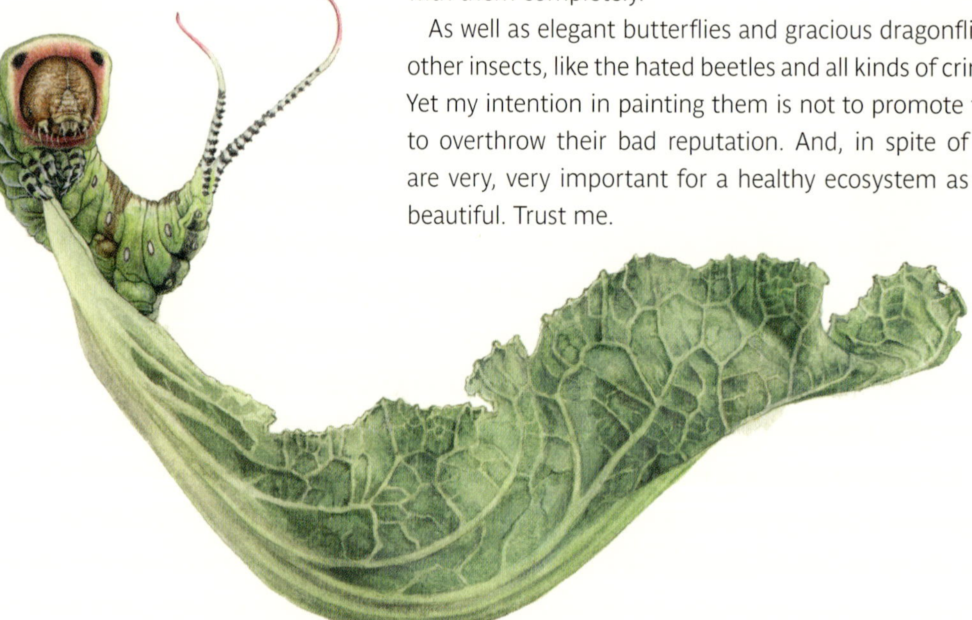

**A puss moth caterpillar,
on balance (2015)**

Insects get a bad reputation. They are often treated as the bad guys regardless of whether they are the culprits or completely innocent. Think of the word 'bugging', for example – it never means doing a favour for someone. And I totally understand why.

My relationship with insects is not a straightforward one – it's rather like a love-hate relationship. And I am not good at handling them.

When I was much younger, I was afraid and felt gross about insects. Caterpillars, especially, were my number one enemy. I screamed when I saw them, but at the same time I couldn't take my eyes off them – while still screaming! My relationship with these small wrigglers was like that for a long time.

However, fascination towards this huge group of creatures increased as I grew into adulthood. Insects are such enchanting creatures and I started seeing them in a very different light. They became my obsession, although I won't declare that I've overcome my complicated relationship with them completely.

As well as elegant butterflies and gracious dragonflies, I also portrayed other insects, like the hated beetles and all kinds of crinkled-nose wigglers. Yet my intention in painting them is not to promote fear. Instead, I wish to overthrow their bad reputation. And, in spite of our screams, they are very, very important for a healthy ecosystem as well as being truly beautiful. Trust me.

Japanese Honeysuckle (2014)
Lonicera japonica

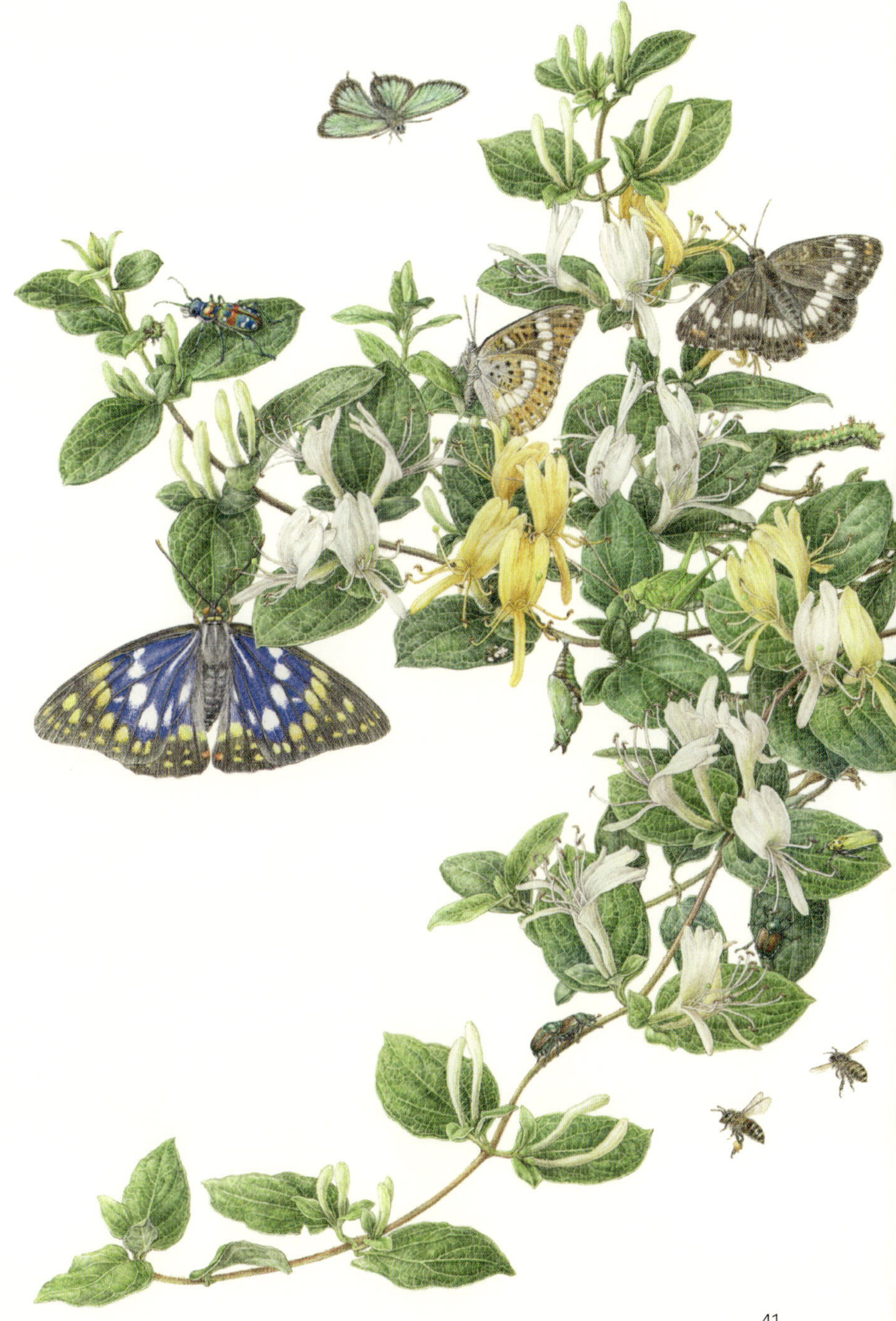

Casanova (2013)
Solanum lycopersicum,
Manduca quinquemaculata

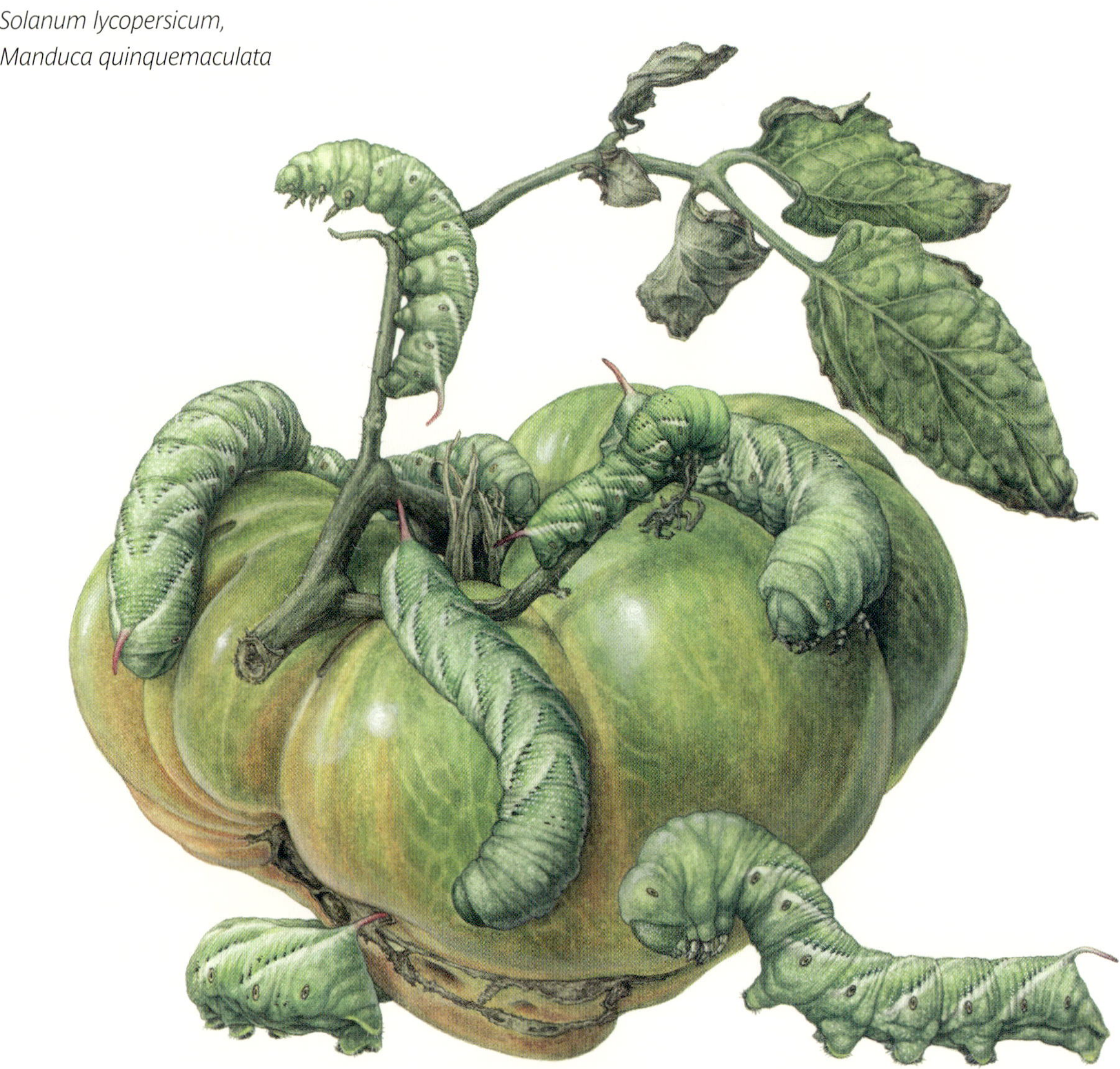

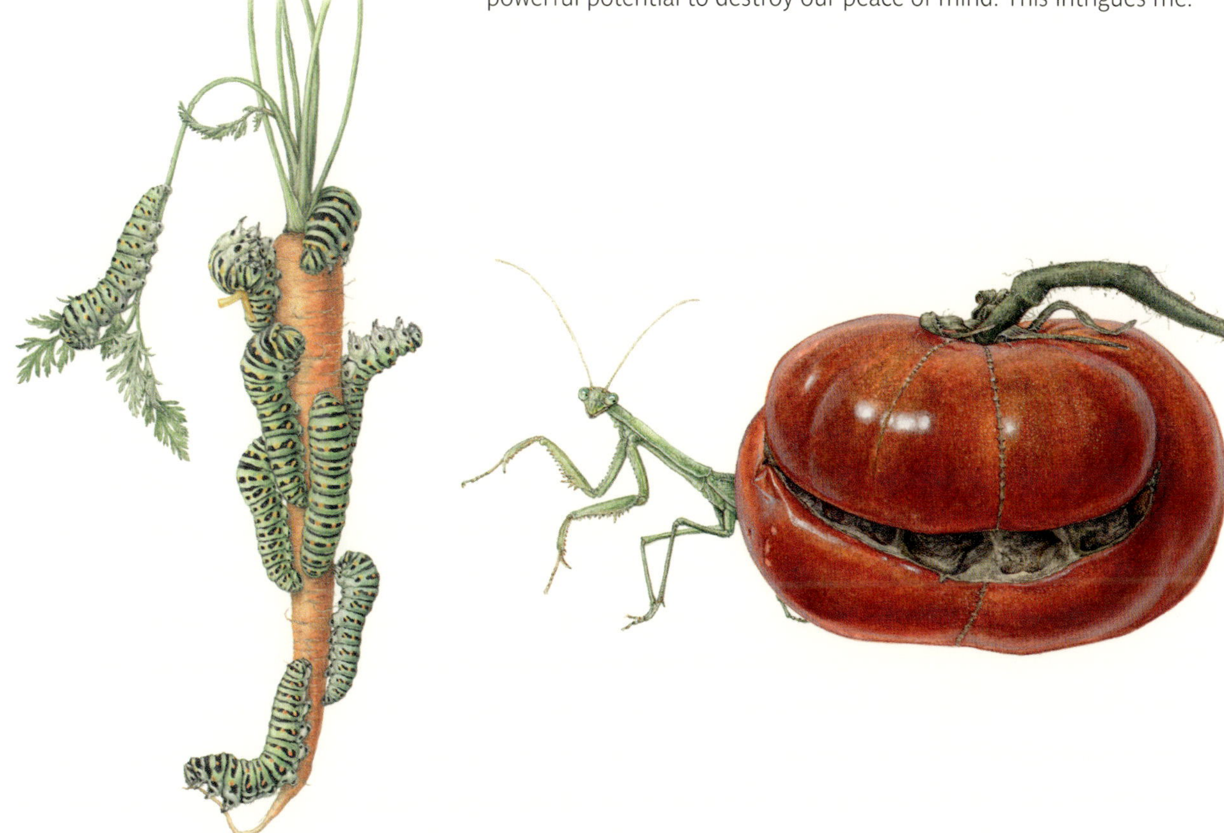

Creep carrot (2013);
A portrait of a heirloom
tomato: Peek-a-boo (2022)

A ladybird in your garden is a charm. If 10 ladybirds help you to protect your plants from aphids, it is a blessing. So how about 100 ladybirds on your favourite tree? Even though these won't harm your plant, they may alarm you, for the 'charm' suddenly metamorphoses into pests – you may think of calling an exterminator. Then, how about seeing millions or even billions of ladybirds in one place? We feel nothing but fear, although a ladybird is just a ladybird. The quantity changes everything. We know it is the same bug, but if it comes in a large quantity, the meaning shifts.

And of course, the impact is much, much larger if it happens with less beautiful insects. Imagine, if a million roses wait for you, you will definitely smile, but not so with some insects. These tiny creatures maintain such powerful potential to destroy our peace of mind. This intrigues me.

A redback spider,
on balance (2015)

Turezure no kusa:
Blackberry
and beetles (2021)

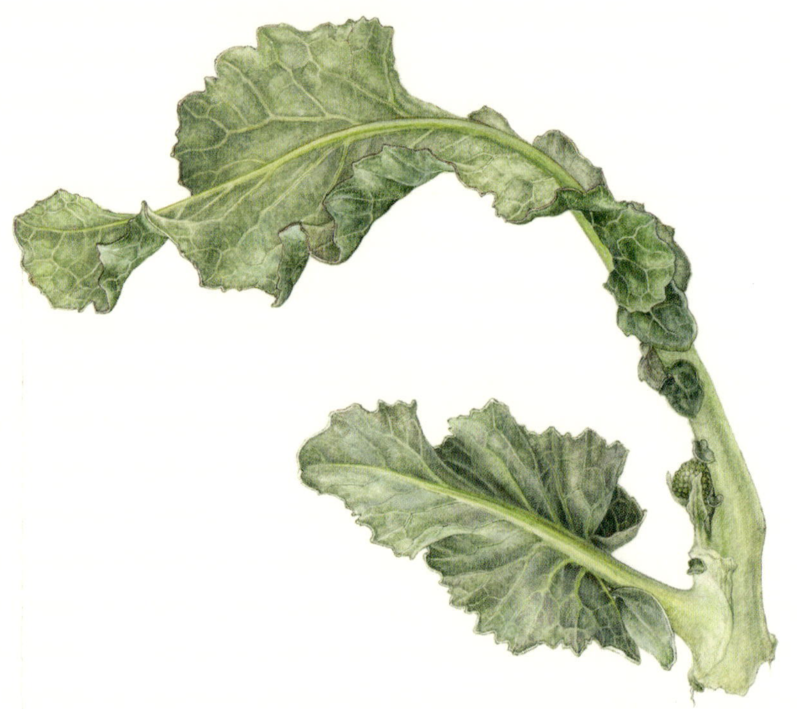

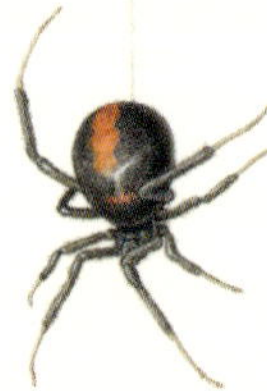

Every early summer, we have so many beetle guests in our backyard, feasting on my blackberry leaves. The blackberry bush seems to not mind at all, so I let them have as much as they wish. But the beetles don't gather together in large numbers. They are polite customers, so normally I'll see one or two beetles on one leaf, and they never fight over one particularly delicious section.

So is this image fabricated? No! It is like an old picture scroll. Each image tells a story and each part of the picture represents a different time. In this case, it is not in the form of a scroll and there's no specific way to read it. Instead, it is a collage of different moments and you can see all the members of the cast at once – beetles, growing summer leaves, ripening berries and also me, observing their dance in nature.

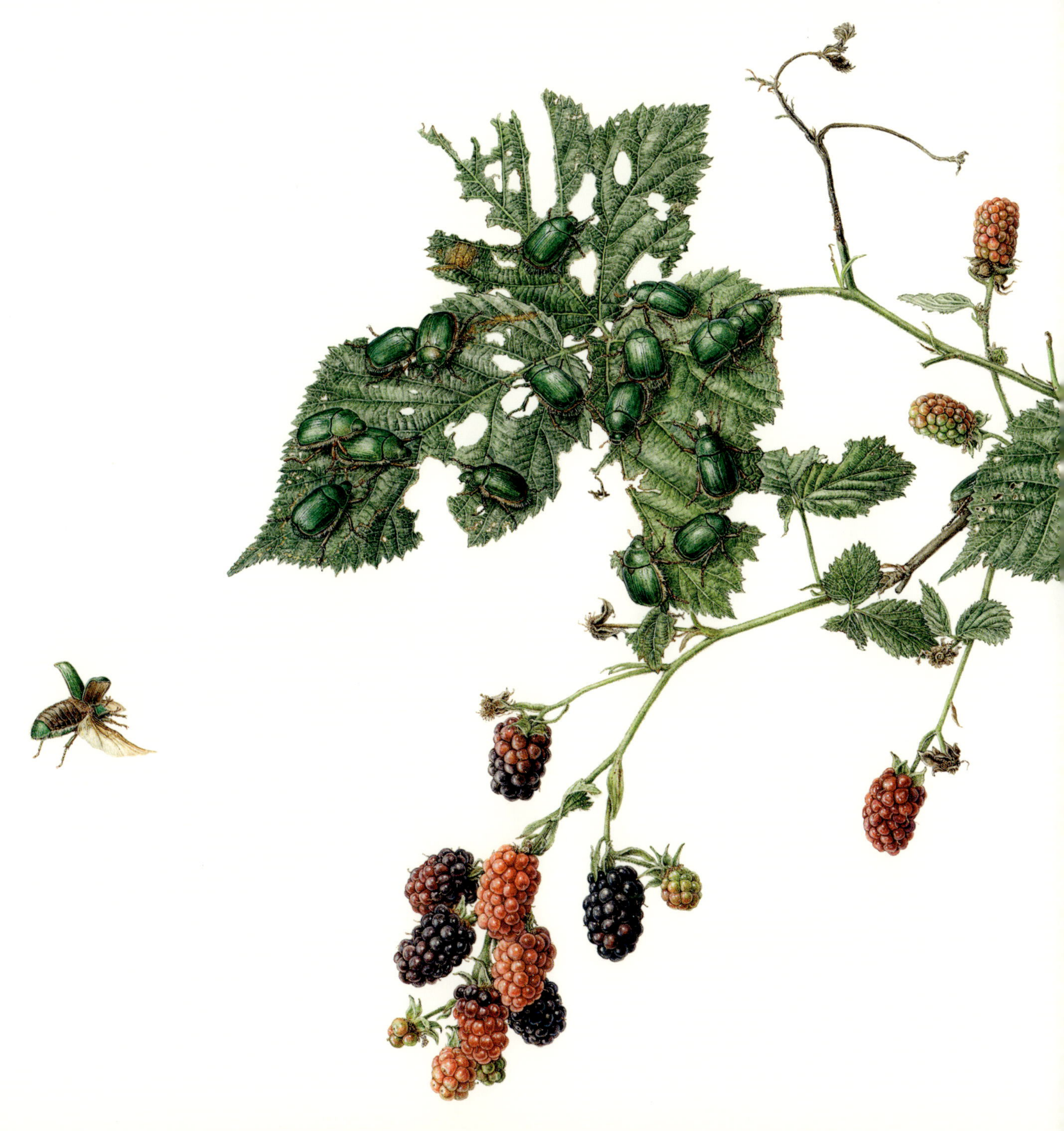

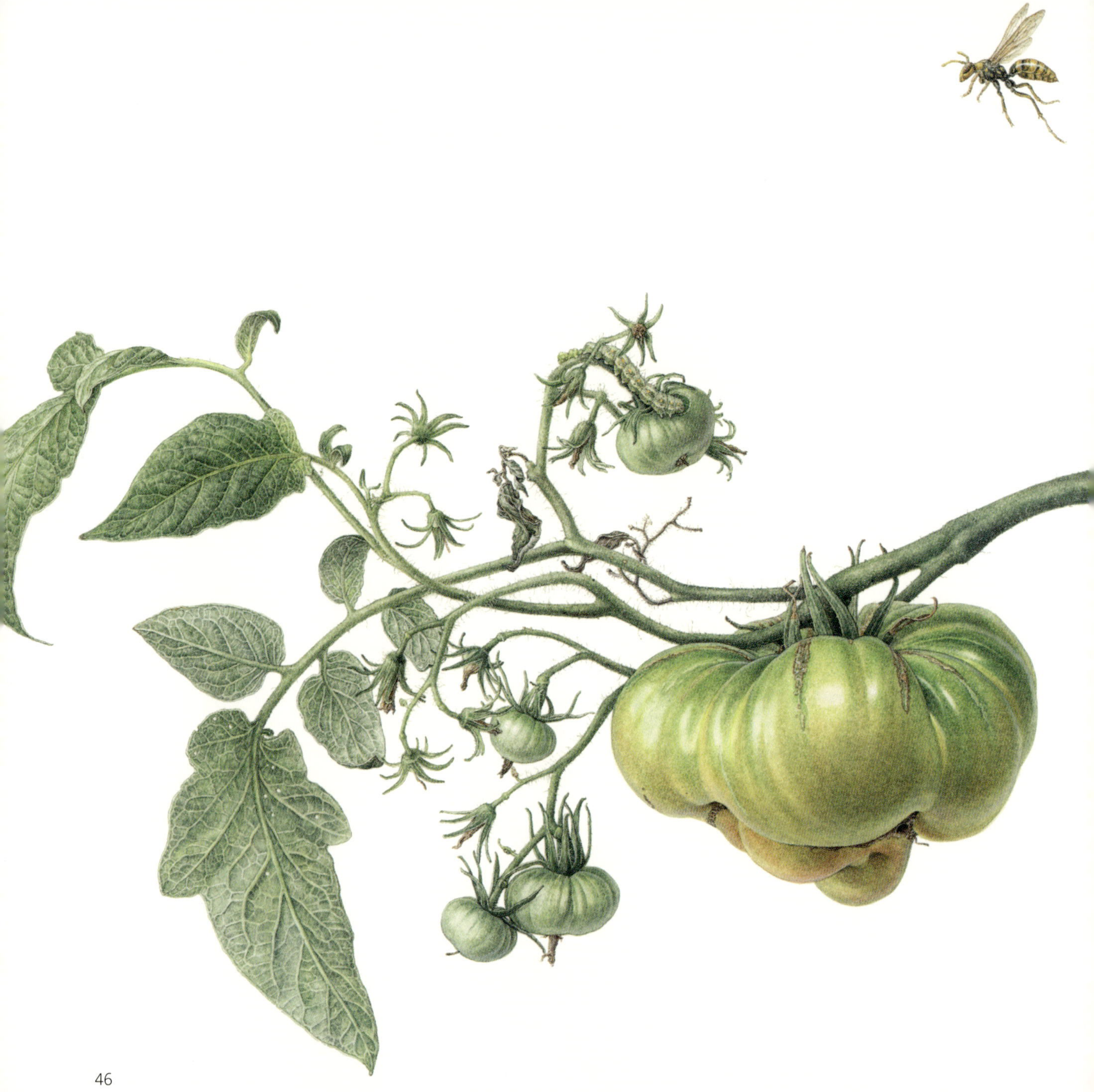

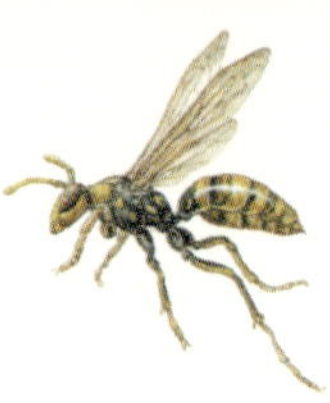

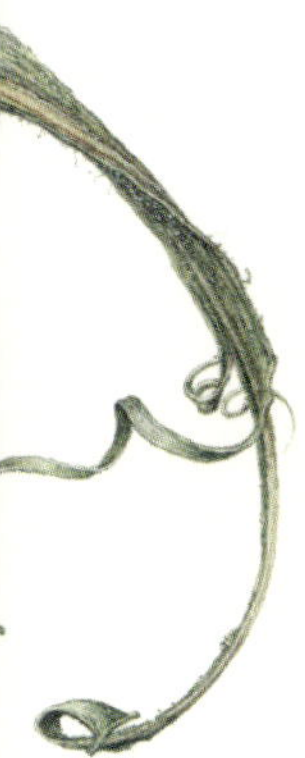

Heirloom tomato (2019–2020)
Animas en el Agua

Bees buzzing, butterflies flapping, caterpillars munching… The sound of insects is peaceful.

Insects interact with plants for many reasons, but it's not always obvious to us why they're there. You can often spot caterpillars on their host plant, feeding happily. If you see them on the ground looking lost, they might have fallen from the host plant nearby. Usually, they are on their way to a sanctuary where they can safely metamorphose into a pupa. Insects know where and when they should be, without learning it at school – they know what to eat, where to find it, where to hide, how to meet a mate, where to lay eggs.

From late spring to early autumn, our backyard turns into a hotspot for wasps and praying mantises. I didn't realise at first that they are after the juicy morsels on my orange tree or tomato plants. Caterpillars and their hunters are always playing hide and seek – it is harsh, come to think of it – and yet, the stronger side doesn't always win. I witnessed a wasp moving up and down in front of a particularly fat caterpillar. The wasp sensed the caterpillar's presence but couldn't spot it. The wasp gave up and flew away to find another victim. Several days later, I couldn't spot the fat caterpillar – it had always been feeding on the same branch. Perhaps the wasp finally caught it or an assassin praying mantis plundered it. Or it may have survived and turned into a chrysalis somewhere safe. I have no way of knowing for sure, but often wonder…

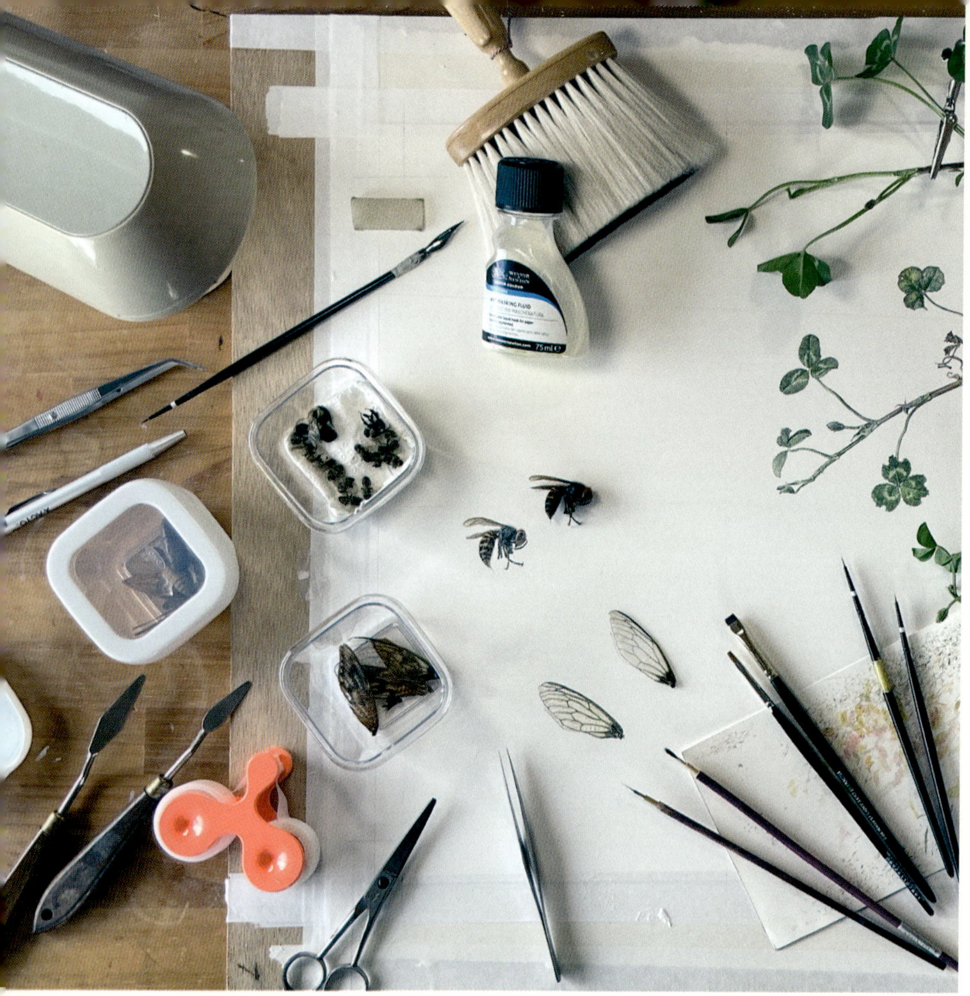

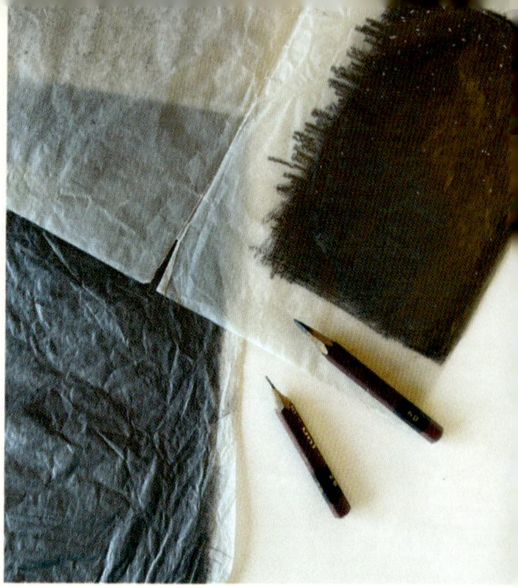

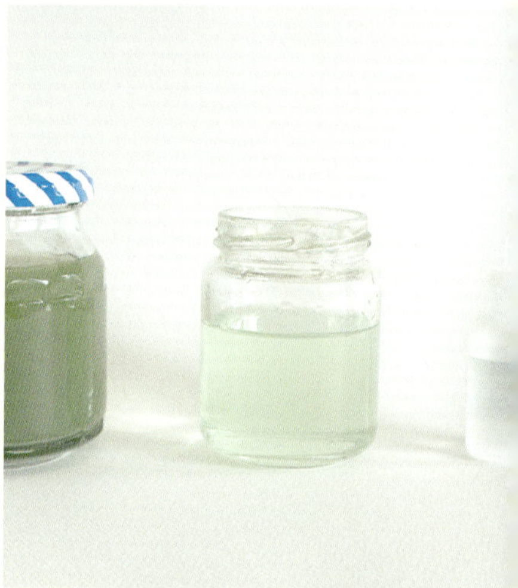

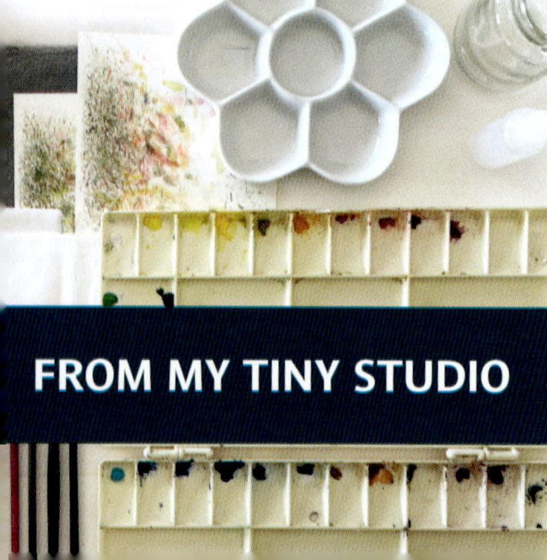

FROM MY TINY STUDIO

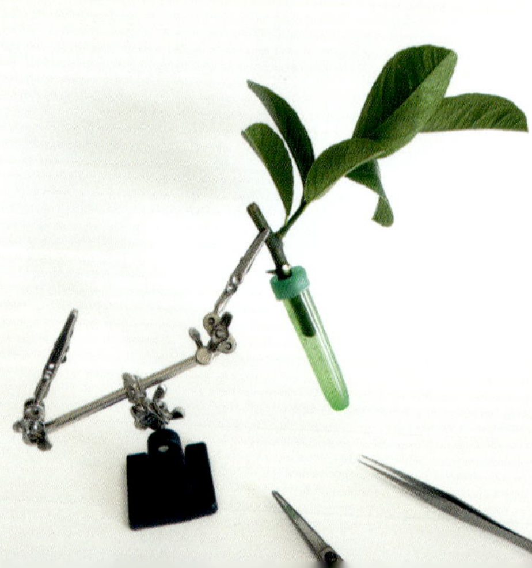

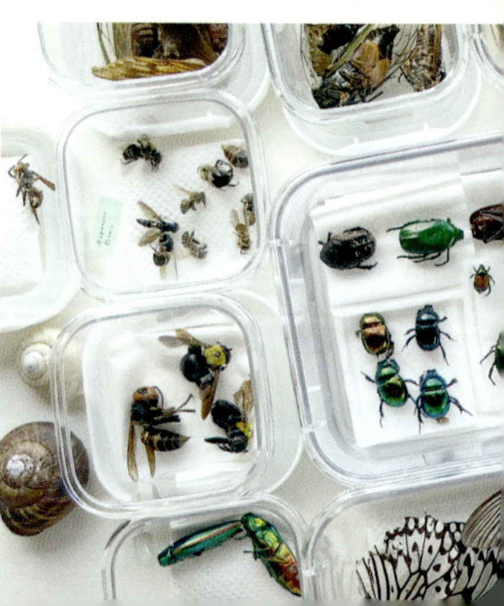

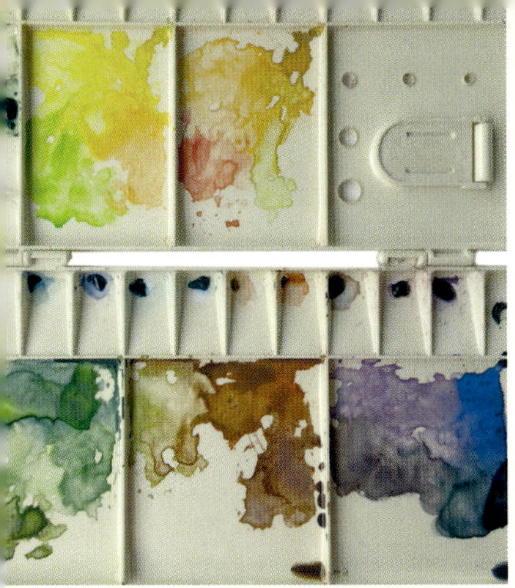
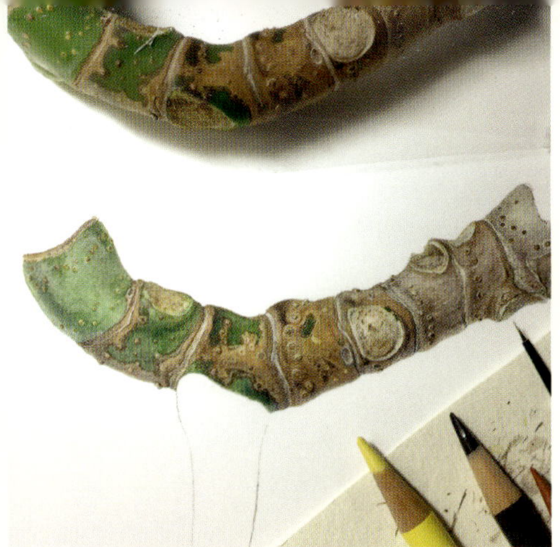
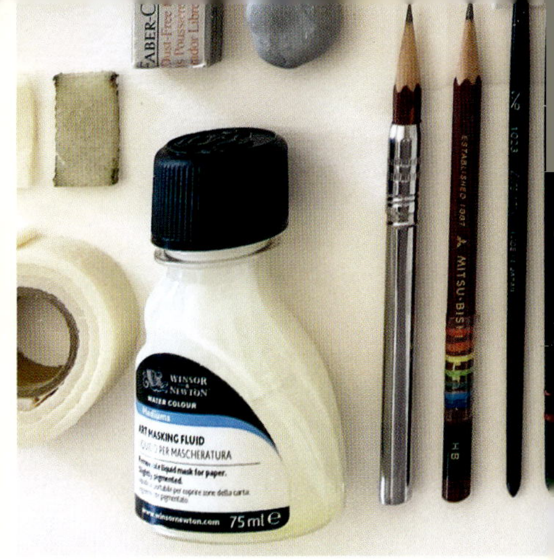

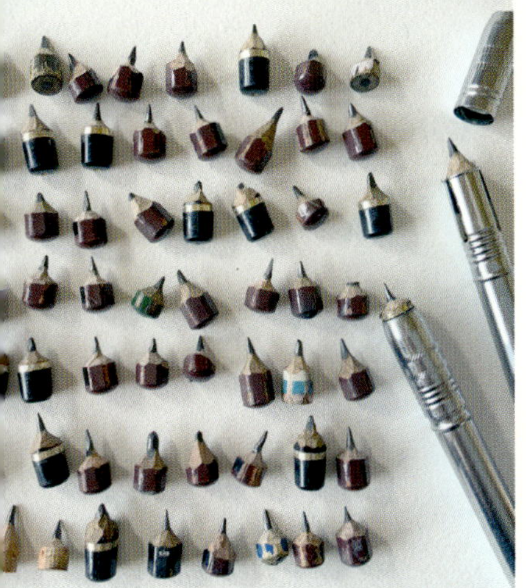

SECRET WEAPONS
What's on my desk

These are the tools I've discovered through a long trial-and-error journey. I consider them my secret weapons! Many were recommended by my artist friends. We all talk to each other about what is best to do what – like exchanging family recipes. The line-up is constantly updated but here are the stars at this moment.

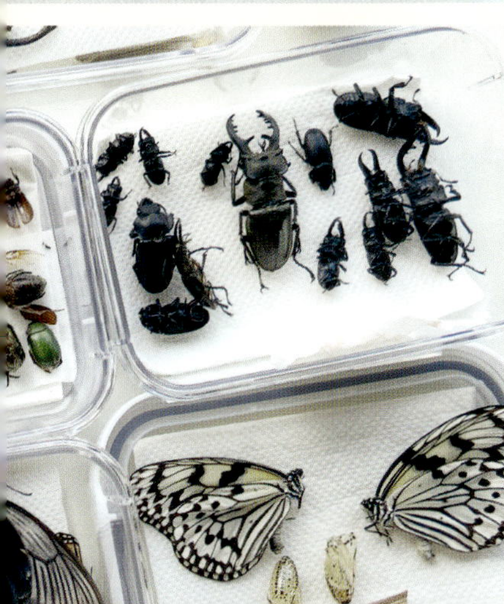
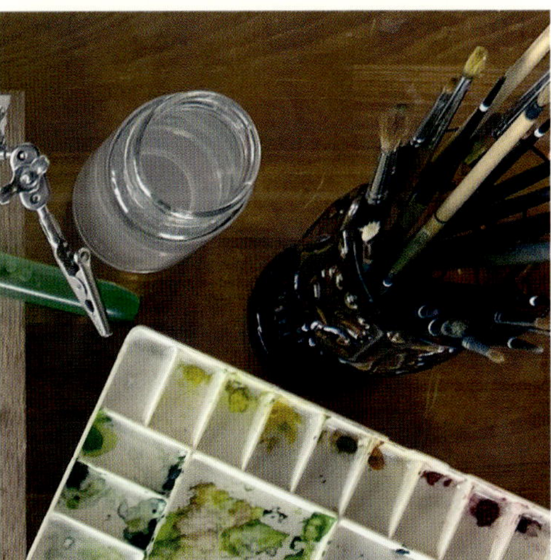
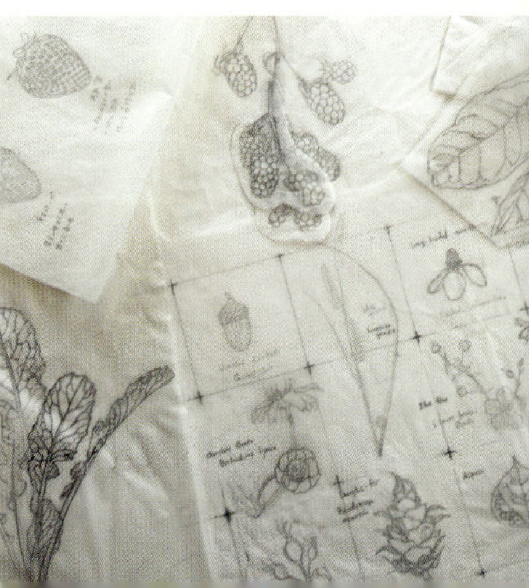

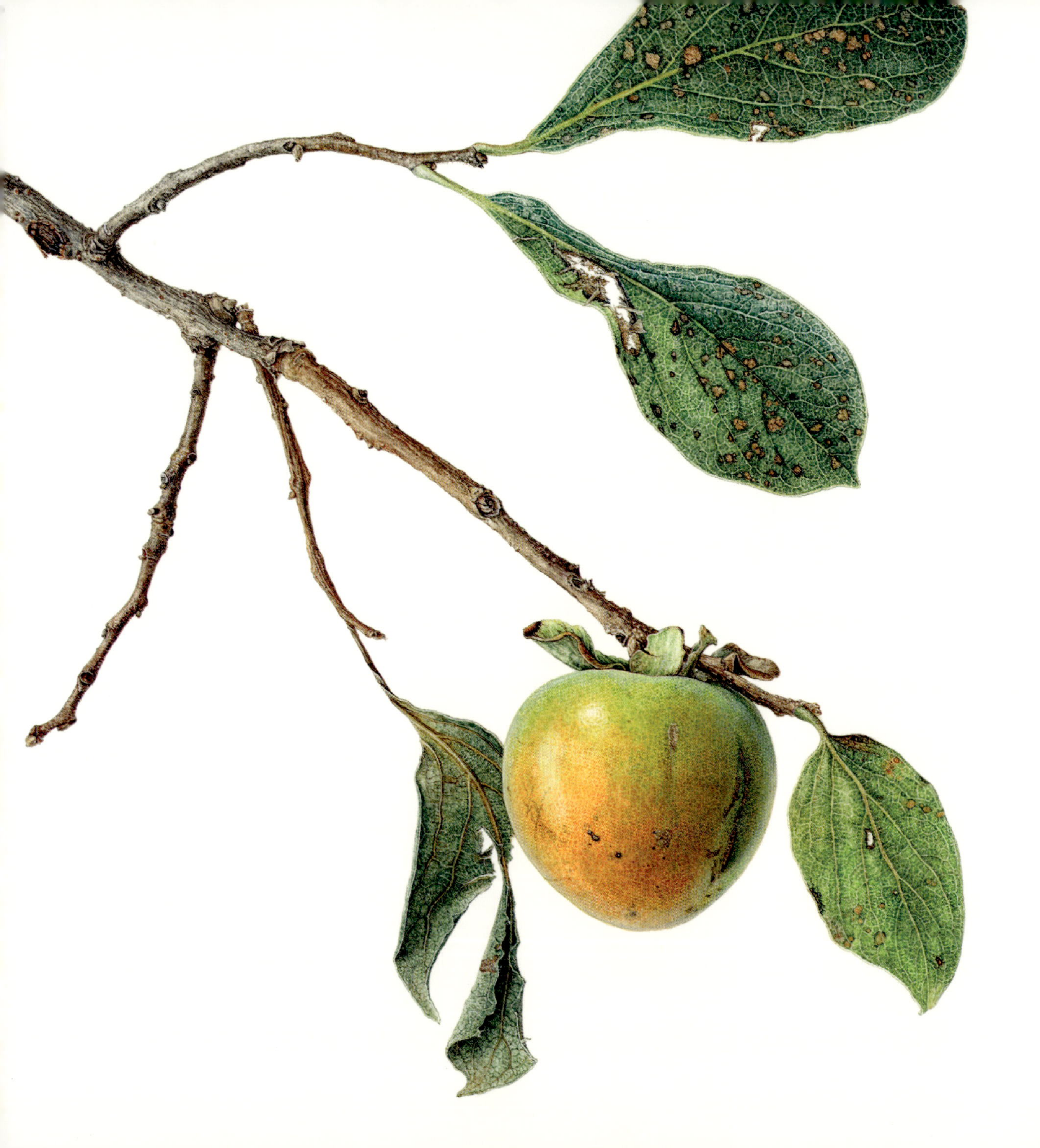

IV. Painting the unpaintable

Depicting my response to my subjects

This may sound weird, but my focus is not to reproduce my subjects with photographic accuracy. What I care most to depict is the excitement and euphoria I feel when I see my subject, the enchanting smell that makes my mouth water or the soft, velvety skin of a plant, inviting me to touch it. It is not hard to draw shapes and colours, but how do I capture the unpaintable elements like the touch, the weight, the smell, and time passing?

Turezure no kusa:
A persimmon on a tree (2021)

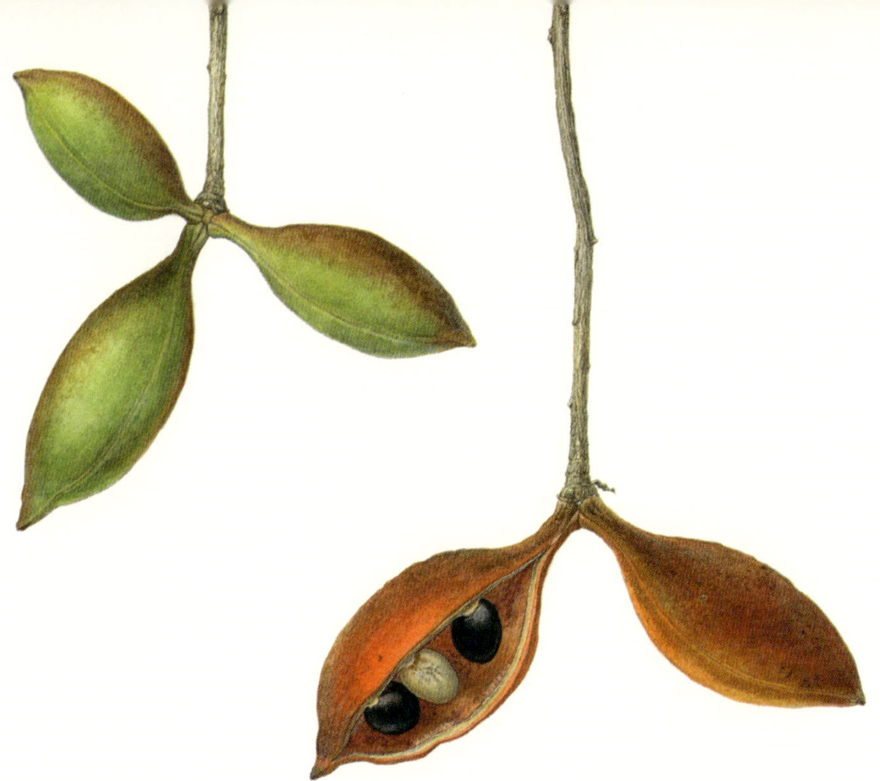

Sterculia rubiginosa (2017)

Nipa palm (2018)
Nypa fruticans

Touch

Eyes give you more clues than you realise. By looking, we can imagine what the texture is like before we actually touch it; soft or hard, rough or smooth, wet or dry, warm or cold. But sometimes our eyes mislead. Super-fine hair on the surface, invisible until we touch it, makes something fuzzier than we thought. Strange – it is so noticeable once spotted. Plants are diverse, so are their textures: sticky, waxy, rubbery, powdery, hairy, burry, warty… All have a reason for their particular texture, and it teaches me more about the plant. Stickiness means there may be nectar inside, warty skin could be hiding tiny oil bubbles underneath.

My final images hold the classified information found by 'touching' with both my eyes and my fingers.

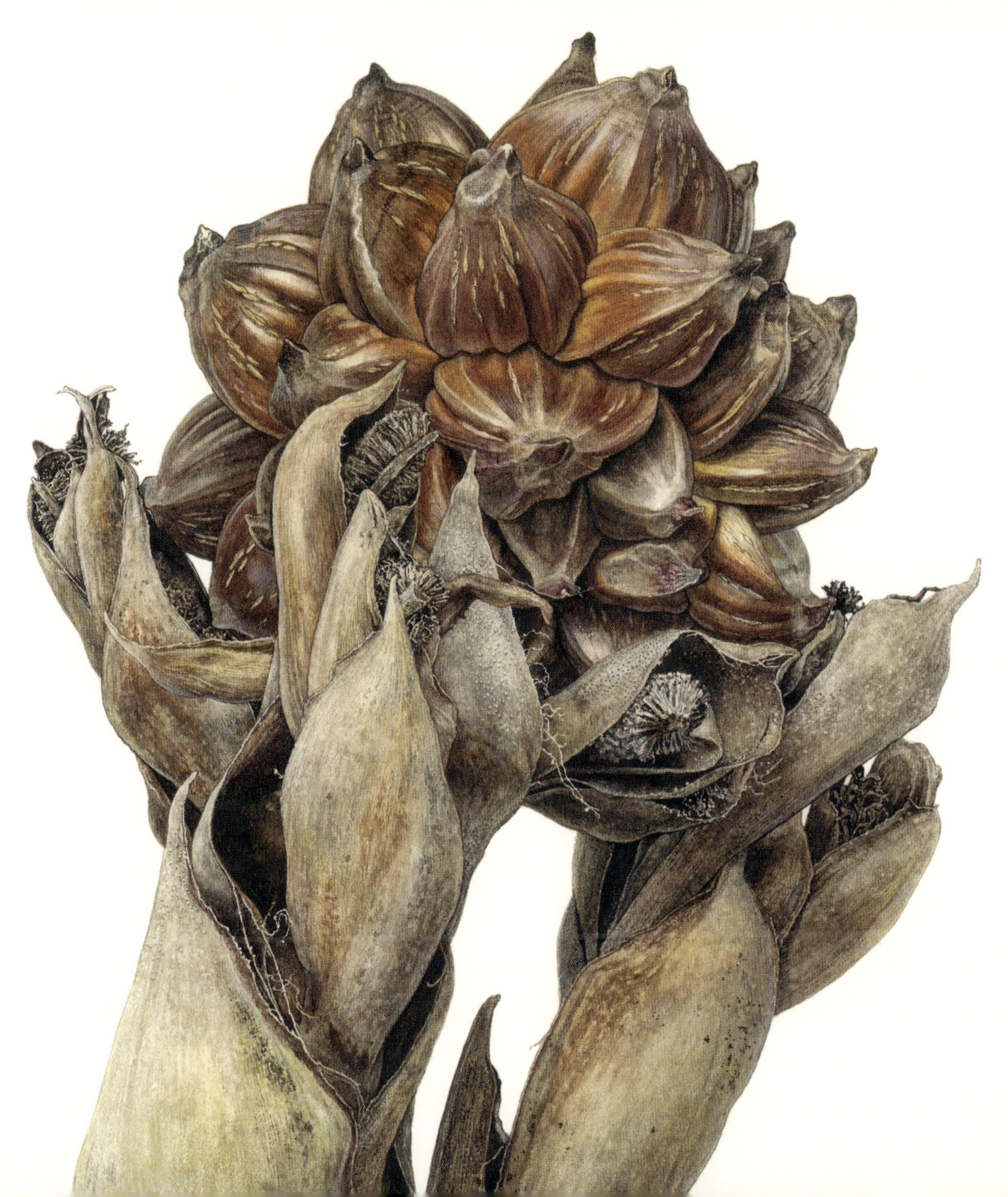

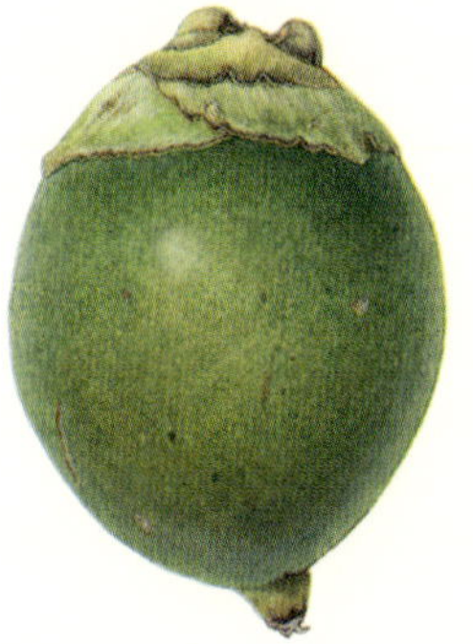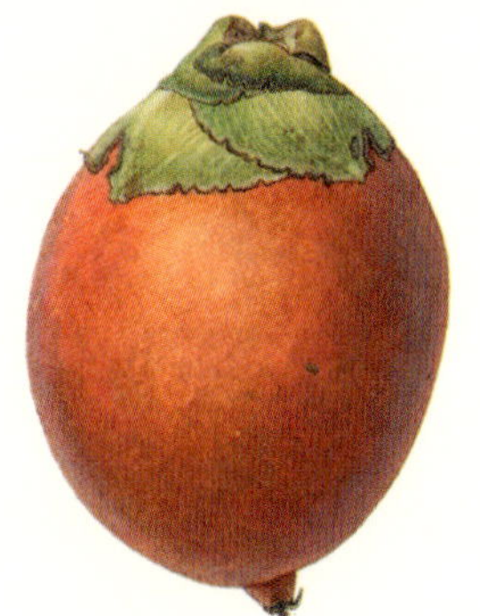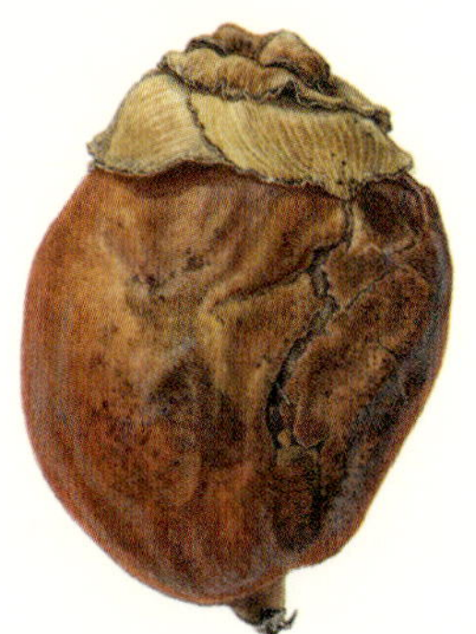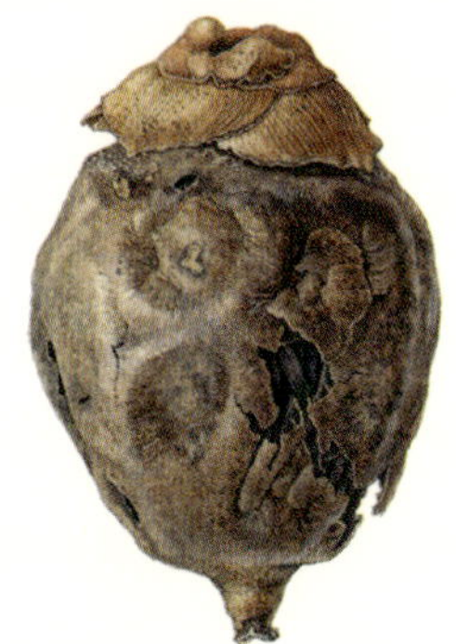

Time

Time is strange. How do we know how much time has passed? I definitely know that time has passed, because the tomato in front of me keeps changing its colour, occasionally its shape. The tomato may then begin to decay and start emitting a stinky smell. This is time for me.

My process is time consuming. I sit beside my subject for a long, long time. I witness the change as time goes by. In the case of flowers, the shift is very dramatic and fast, but stems and leaves last much longer. Yet it is also unpredictable – sometimes a flower decays very slowly and a leaf dries up overnight. I know this sounds like nonsense, but I just wish they would let me know their schedule before we start working together.

Foxtail palm fruit
Wodyetia bifurcata (2017)

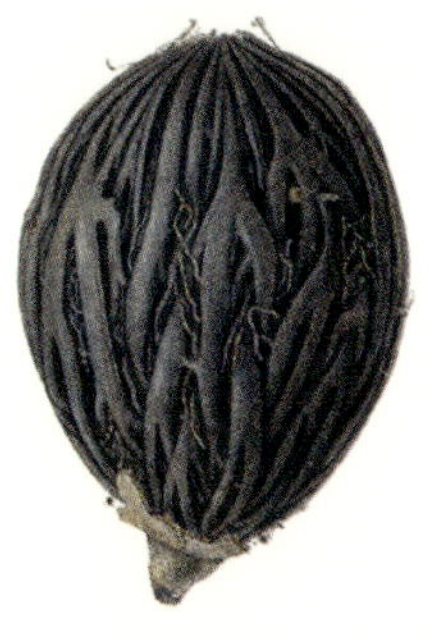

When I started painting this tiny tomato, it was yellowish green, but I knew it was ready to ripen and turn red. I started from the left side – I remember it was still a strong green colour with a yellow-orange background. While I was chasing the left side, the tomato was gaining that reddish tint, little by little. By the time I reached the right side, the tomato was fully red, just leaving a bit of green on top. My painting looked like a rainbow-coloured tomato, but it would never have had that graduation of colour all at once. In fact, it was like a documentary – from the left side to the right side, each part recorded at a different time. So 'time' is there, in a painting.

I understand that a photograph is the art that captures a fraction of time, freezing the moment. On the other hand, my subject is frozen with a certain period of time within it. My painting contains 'time'.

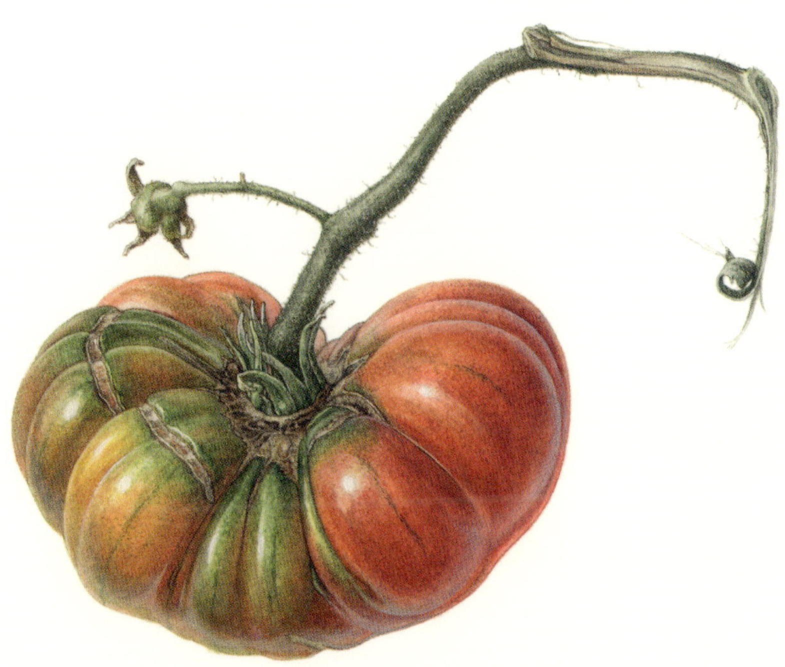

A portrait of a heirloom tomato:
A little pretty pleats (2015)

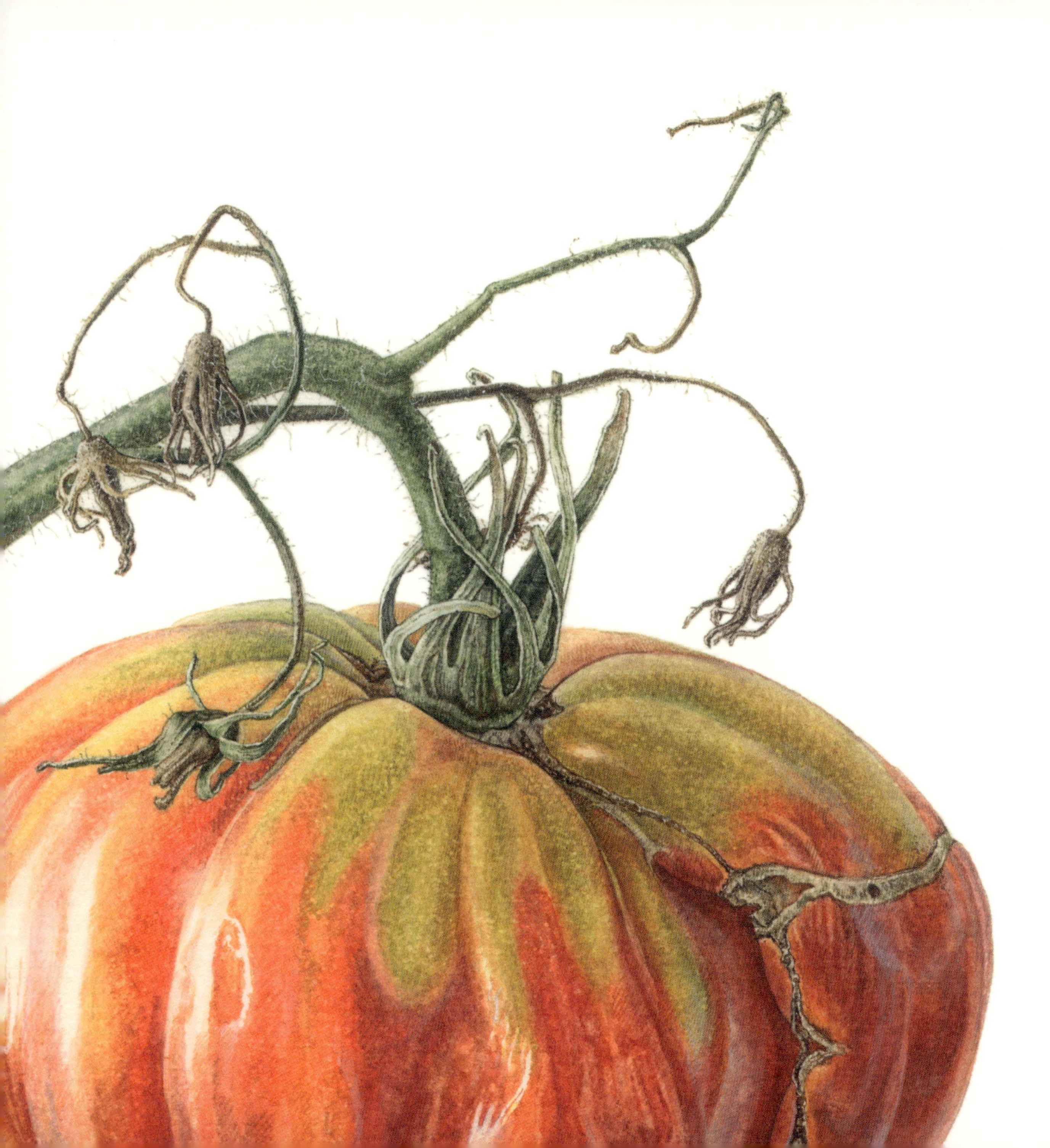

Weight

The tomato weighed 648 grams, that's about 23 ounces. Tomato stems are really tough. Imagine holding that heavy fruit 24/7 and, if it isn't picked that day, it will be even heavier the next day. Picking the tomato by its stem with my fingers hurt. My knuckles turned white just holding it.

On the other hand, the half-dried tomato leaves were very light and fragile – as were the saga tree seed pods, making a dried, crinkling noise every time I changed angle to find the best view. I had to be extra careful when I handled them because a slight wrong touch would easily break them.

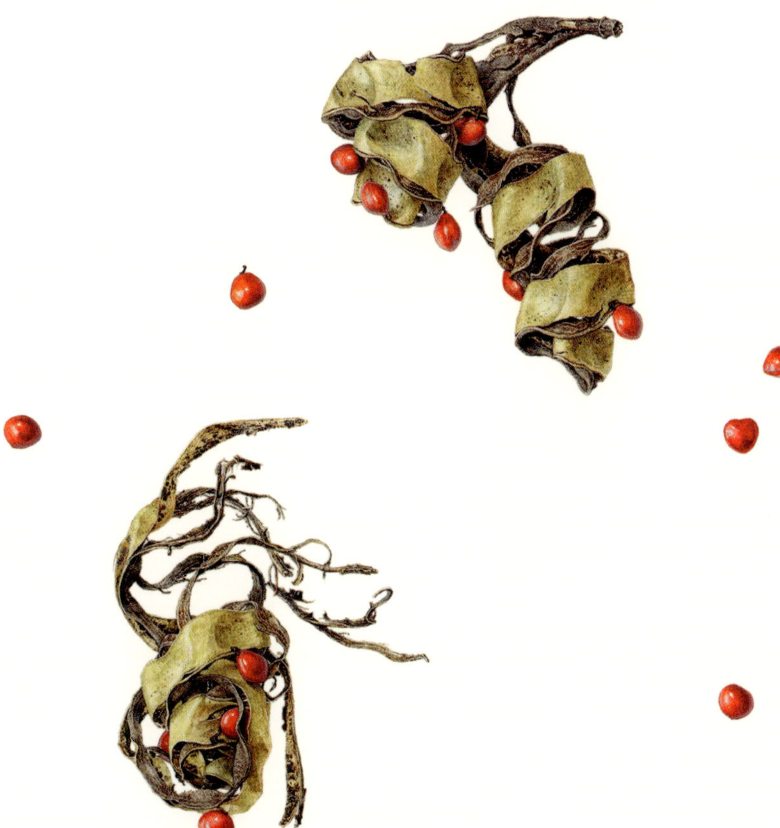

A portrait of a heirloom tomato:
Fashion Editor (2016)

Saga seed pod (2022)
Adenanthera pavonina

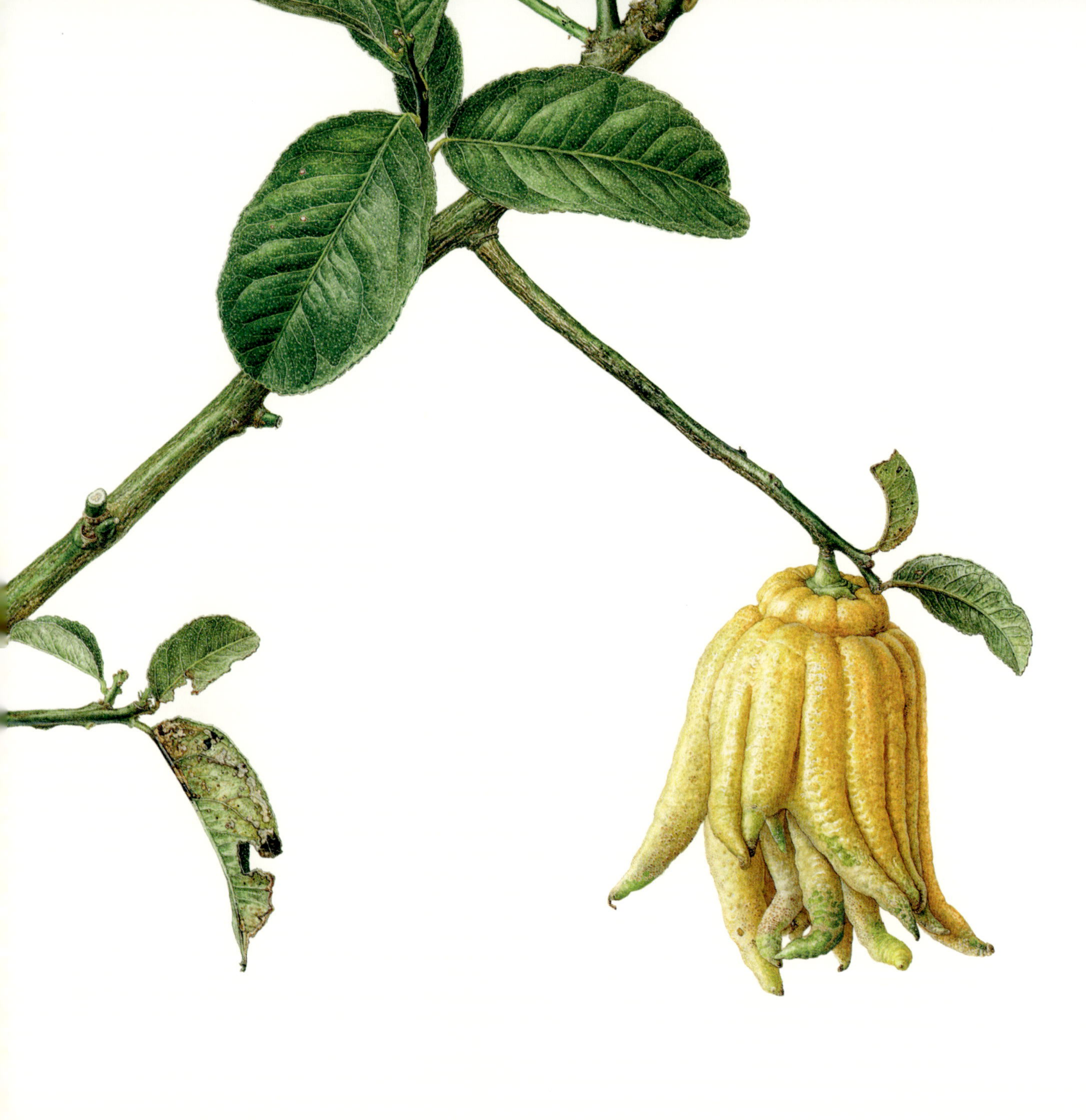

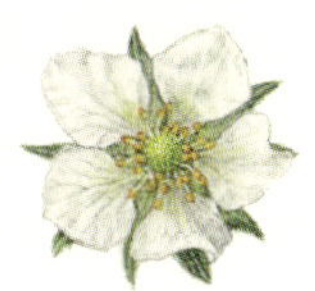

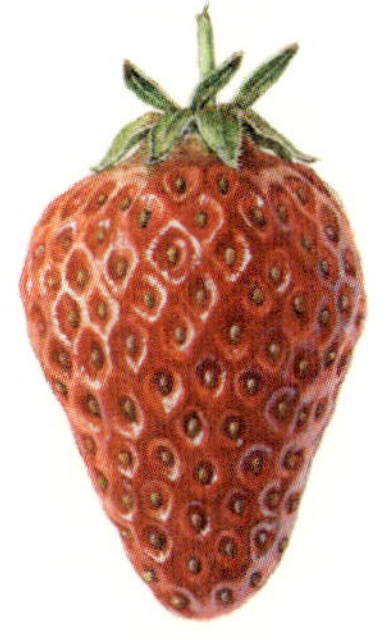

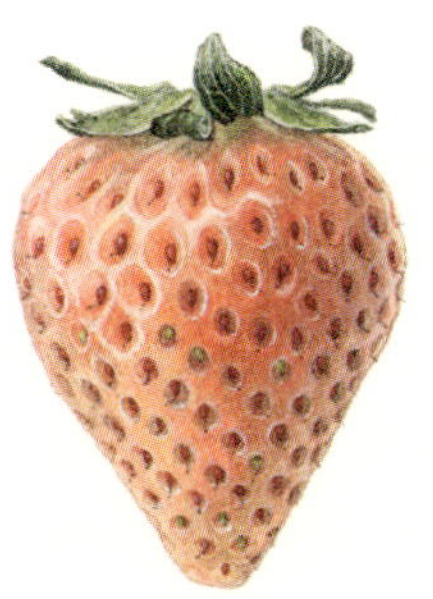

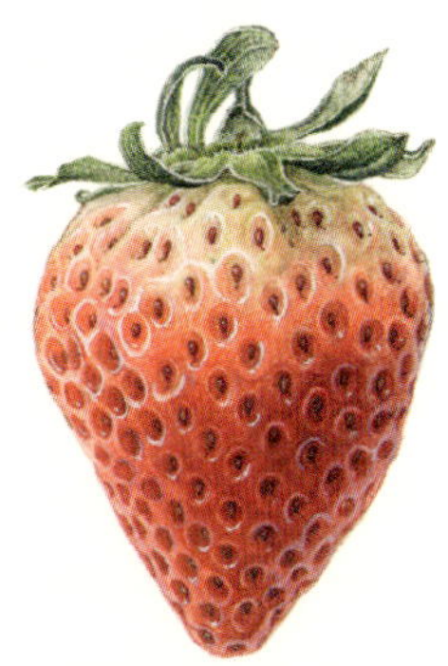

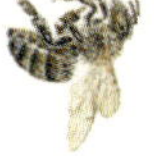

Smell

The citrus scent of the Buddha's hand plant is heavenly. Each morning, when I open the studio door, the hint of its seductive aroma overflows from the room. It is not a strong smell, but somehow powerfully remarkable. Strangely, the Buddha's hand scent calms me down, as if I am sitting in a semi-dark temple.

Likewise, strawberries have an appealing smell, though the fragrance intrigues my appetite more than soothing my feelings. There are about 70 cultivars, possibly more, of strawberries in Japan. You could say we are possessed by strawberries. The pale pink strawberry in the middle has the sweetest aroma, blackmailing me to bite it before finishing the painting. I did follow the devil's whisper, but picked one from the spares – I bought a box of the pale pink ones. No harm done, but it didn't taste as good as the bewitching scent.

Turezure no kusa:
A Buddha's hand on a tree (2022)

Strawberries, flower, and a honey-bee (2019)

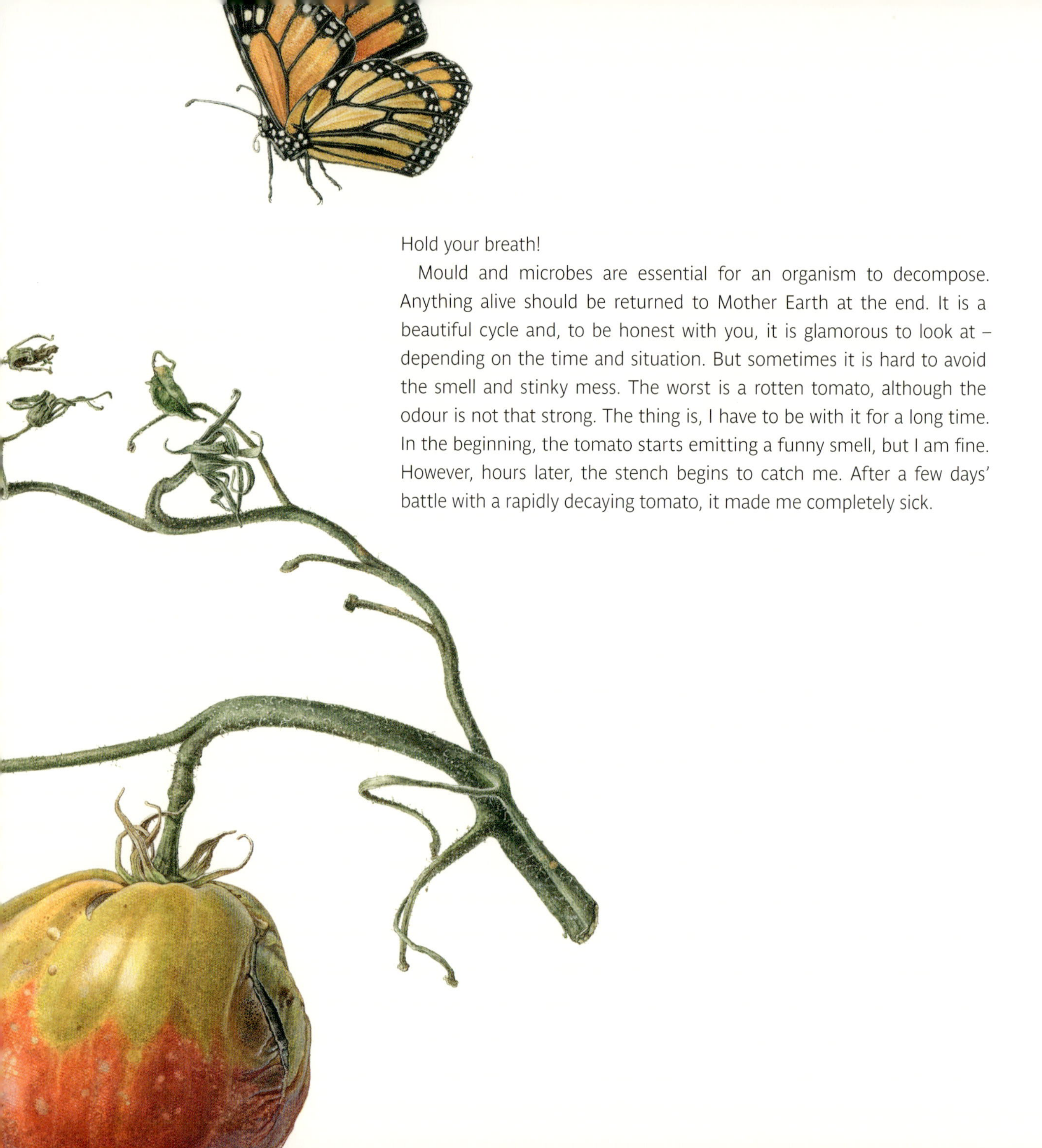

Hold your breath!

Mould and microbes are essential for an organism to decompose. Anything alive should be returned to Mother Earth at the end. It is a beautiful cycle and, to be honest with you, it is glamorous to look at – depending on the time and situation. But sometimes it is hard to avoid the smell and stinky mess. The worst is a rotten tomato, although the odour is not that strong. The thing is, I have to be with it for a long time. In the beginning, the tomato starts emitting a funny smell, but I am fine. However, hours later, the stench begins to catch me. After a few days' battle with a rapidly decaying tomato, it made me completely sick.

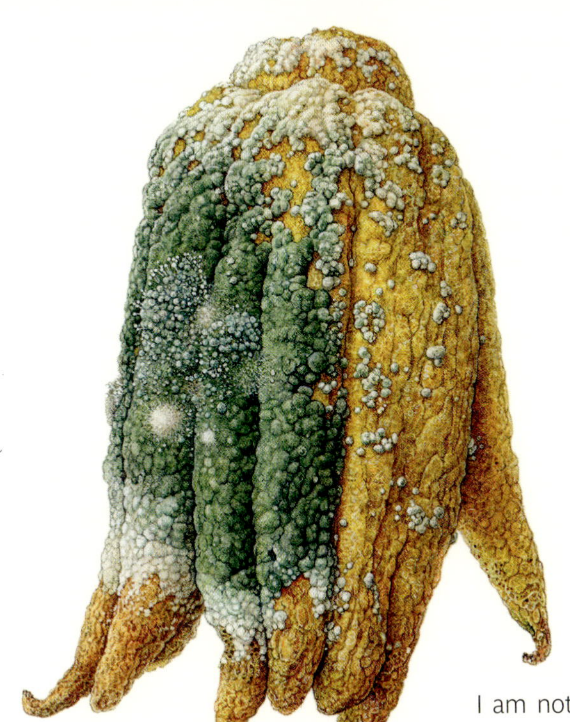

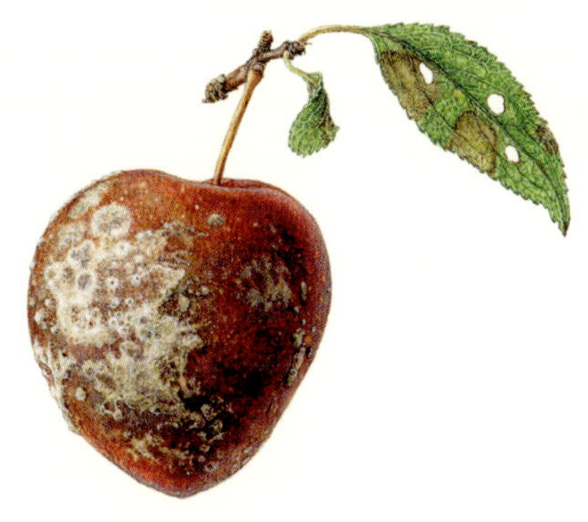

A half-rotten tomato
and a butterfly (2018)

Turezure no kusa:
Mould-covered Buddha's
hand (2022)

Turezure no kusa:
Mould-covered plum (2020)

I am not only a trash saver, but also a keeper, as well as a very bad maintenance manager. Naturally, my subject decays, each fragment rotting away differently. Some parts dry out, some get covered in mould. But miraculously, a true hidden treasure emerges among the half-decomposed chaos.

The Buddha's hand was found covered with white, snowy mould. While I was portraying it from one side, I let it grow and I enjoyed the change. It turned into a thick, green, carpet-like mould. The chase wasn't easy, as the mould expanded very quickly, but with one wrong move it could easily collapse and melt away. The mould is more sensitive than we think. I put it in a glass lasagne dish and covered it with an acrylic sheet to observe so that the mould wouldn't be disturbed. And I didn't desire to inhale any hyphae for health reasons, but I could still smell it through three layers of masks. It was a strange, sweet-smelling scent. I am sure it was mixed with the soothing, fresh aroma of citrus, but it seemed that the mould itself had the sugary scent. There was a bit of toxic sweetness about it too.

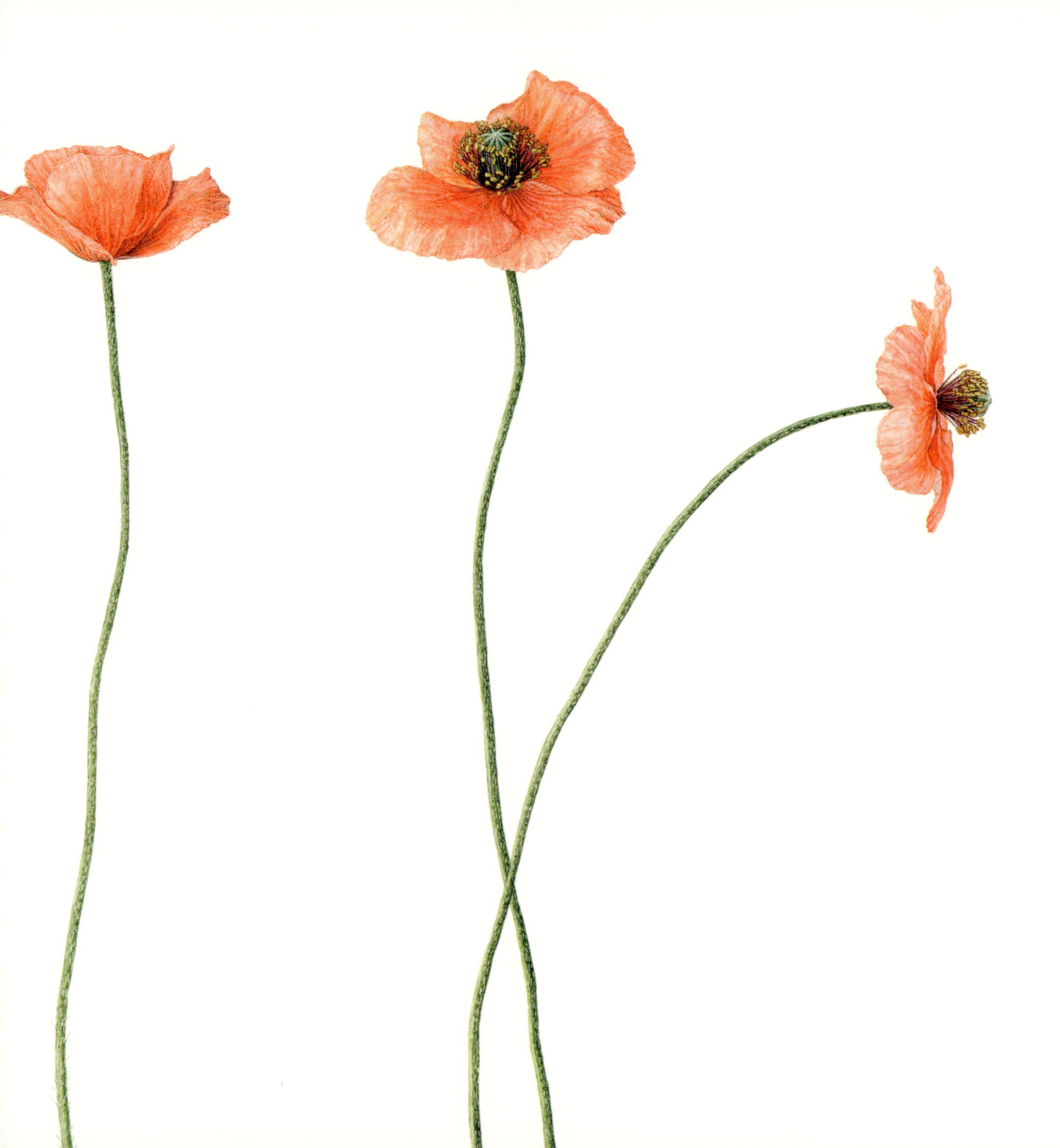

Dreaming

This amazingly battered-looking leaf reminded me of a long life – the miseries and satisfactions of being alive. But I was also clearly aware that it was reflecting my mood at that time. Our moods lead us to a completely different set of responses depending on the circumstances. We humans are fabulous creatures who can see things that don't exist in front of us, feeling them with our mind's eyes. I think this is human nature. If you see a pale orange flower dancing in the wind, it may remind you of the pale orange dress you wore when you were small. Suddenly, the good old memories along with bittersweet feelings flood inside you. Just a tiny street flower can trigger your deep memories, taking you back to the past and filling you up with strong emotions.

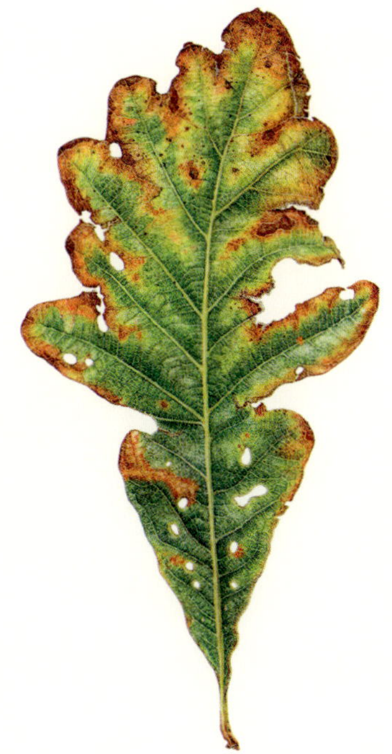

Turezure no kusa:
Three poppies (2021)

Aged white oak leaf (2021)

A portrait of a heirloom tomato

It may be my imagination, but often I see characters in my subjects, especially in heirloom tomatoes. These one-of-a-kind features are telling me stories. I know it is strange. A tomato does not have a character, yet I cannot resist finding a very distinct persona in it. I see smiles, sneaks, boldness, successes, weakness, kindness and sadness. I cannot help it. I think this is us. Our imaginations fly like butterflies, consciously or unconsciously.

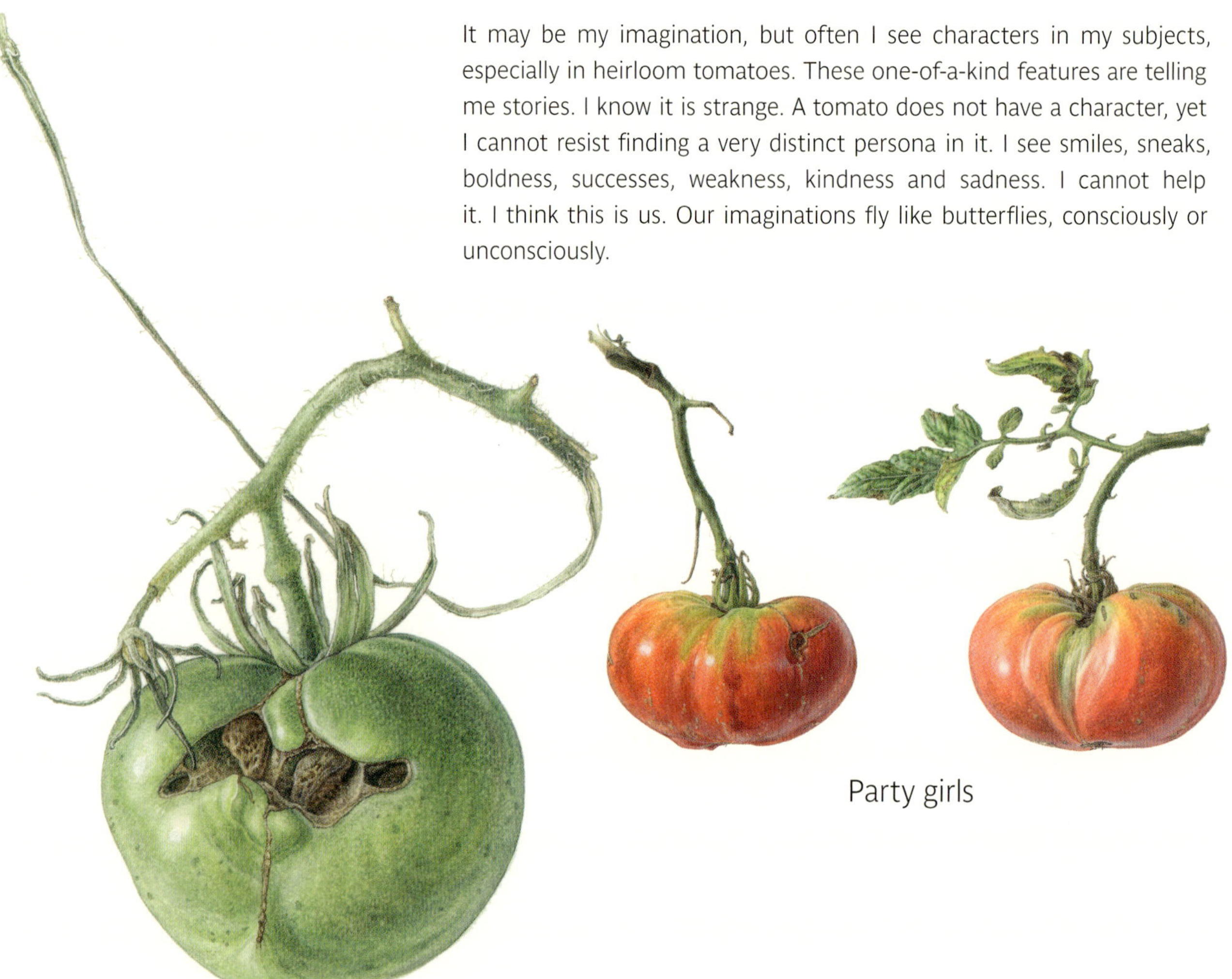

Party girls

Weeping baby

A portrait of a heirloom tomato:
Weeping baby (2015);
Party girls (2015)

A portrait of a heirloom tomato:
Yakuza Brothers (2009);
The Smiths (2011)

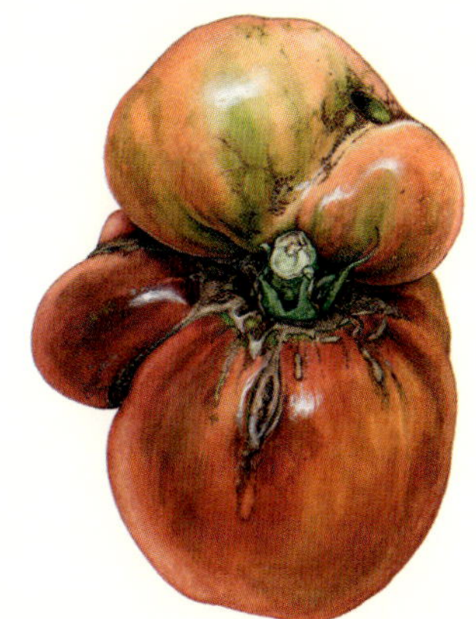
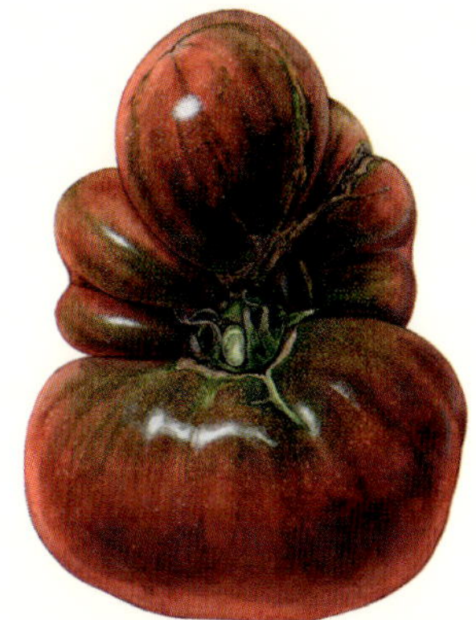

Yakuza brothers

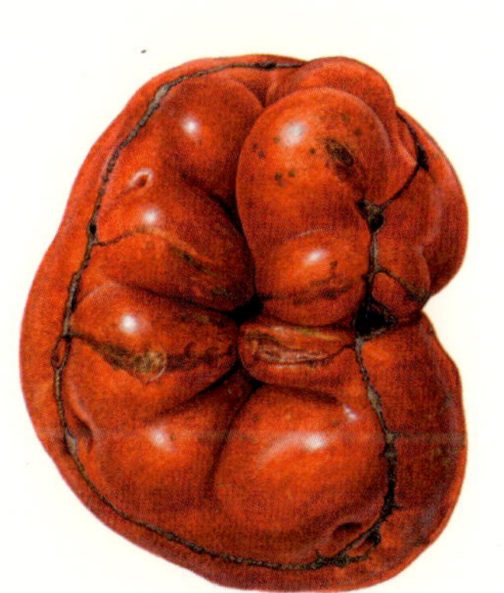
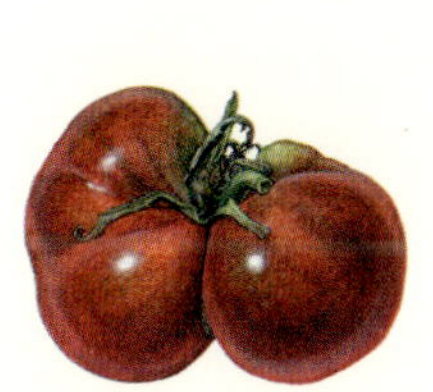
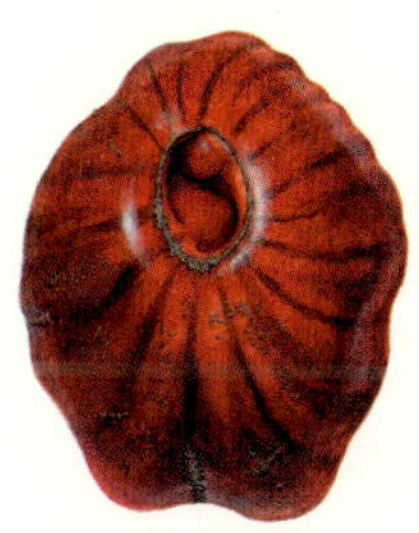
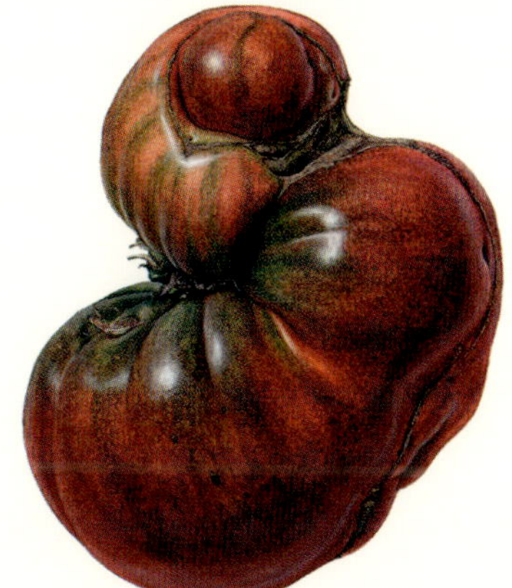

The Smiths

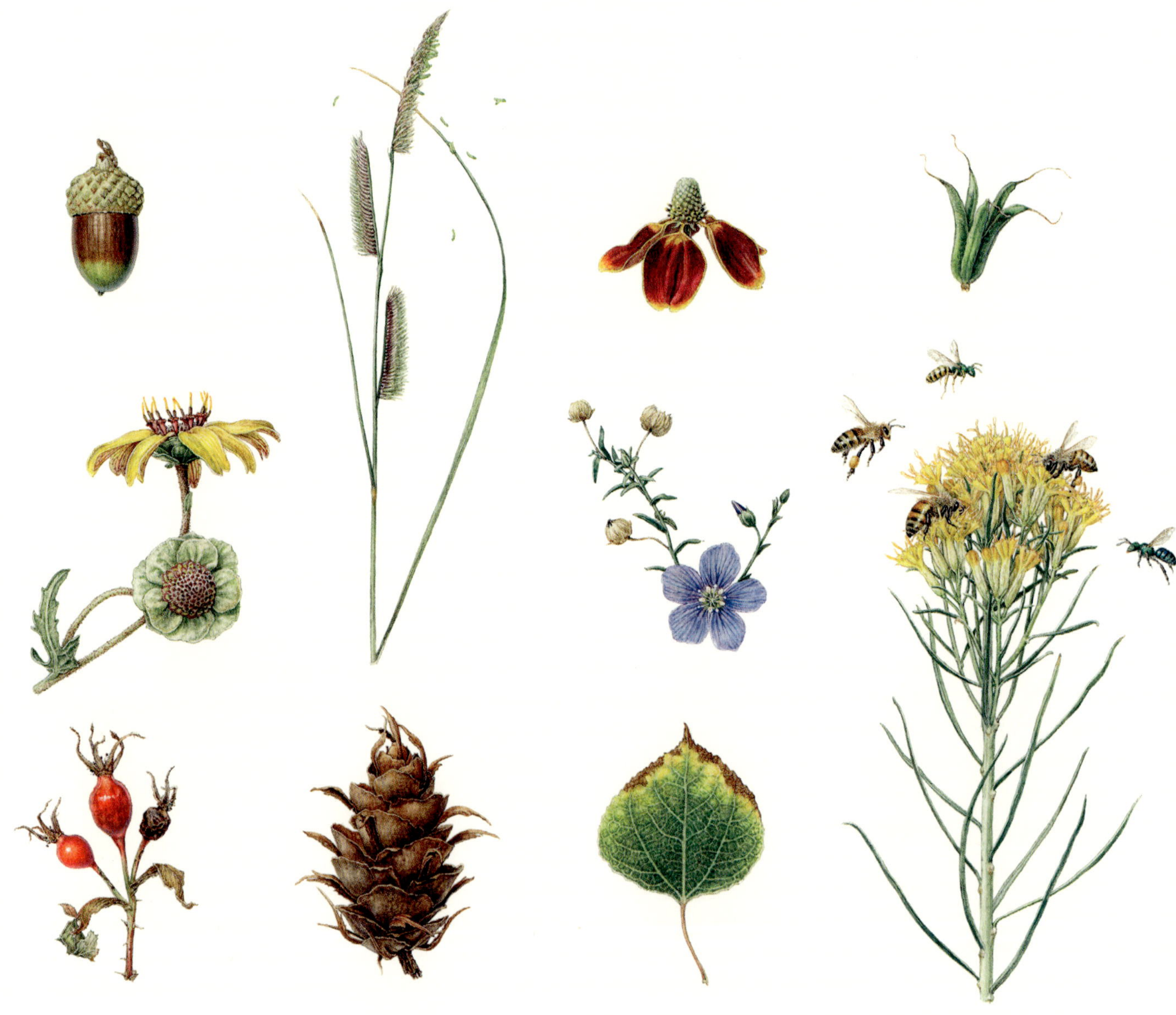

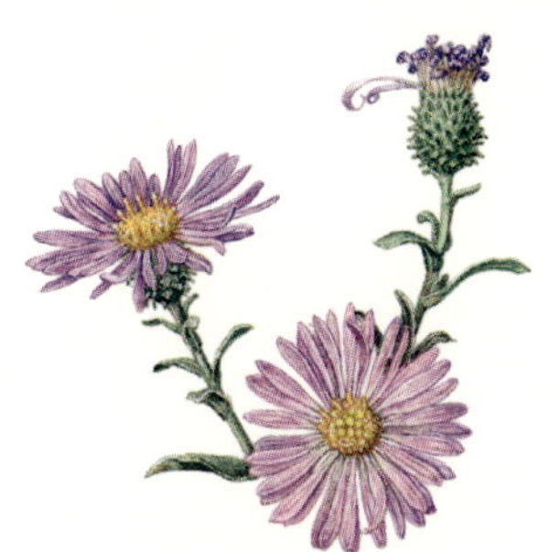

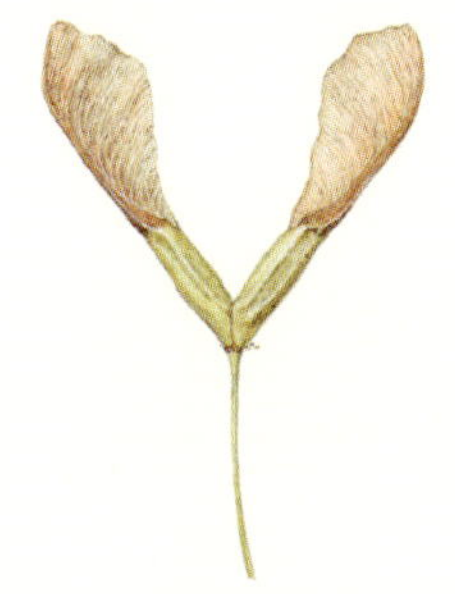

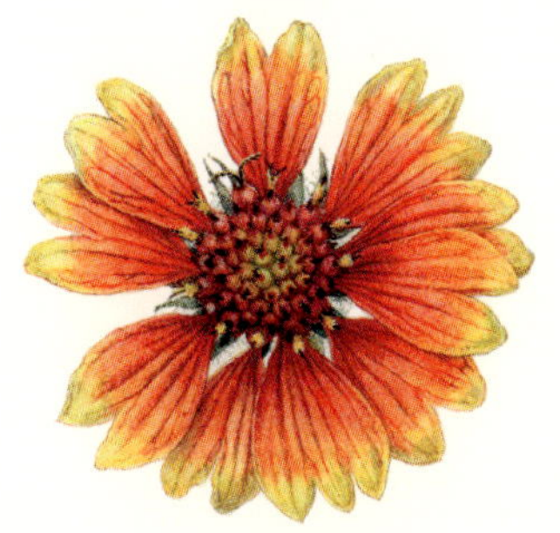

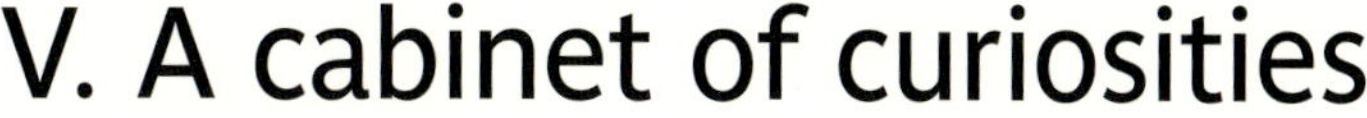

V. A cabinet of curiosities

My collections

Diary: Denver Botanic Gardens (Fall 2018)

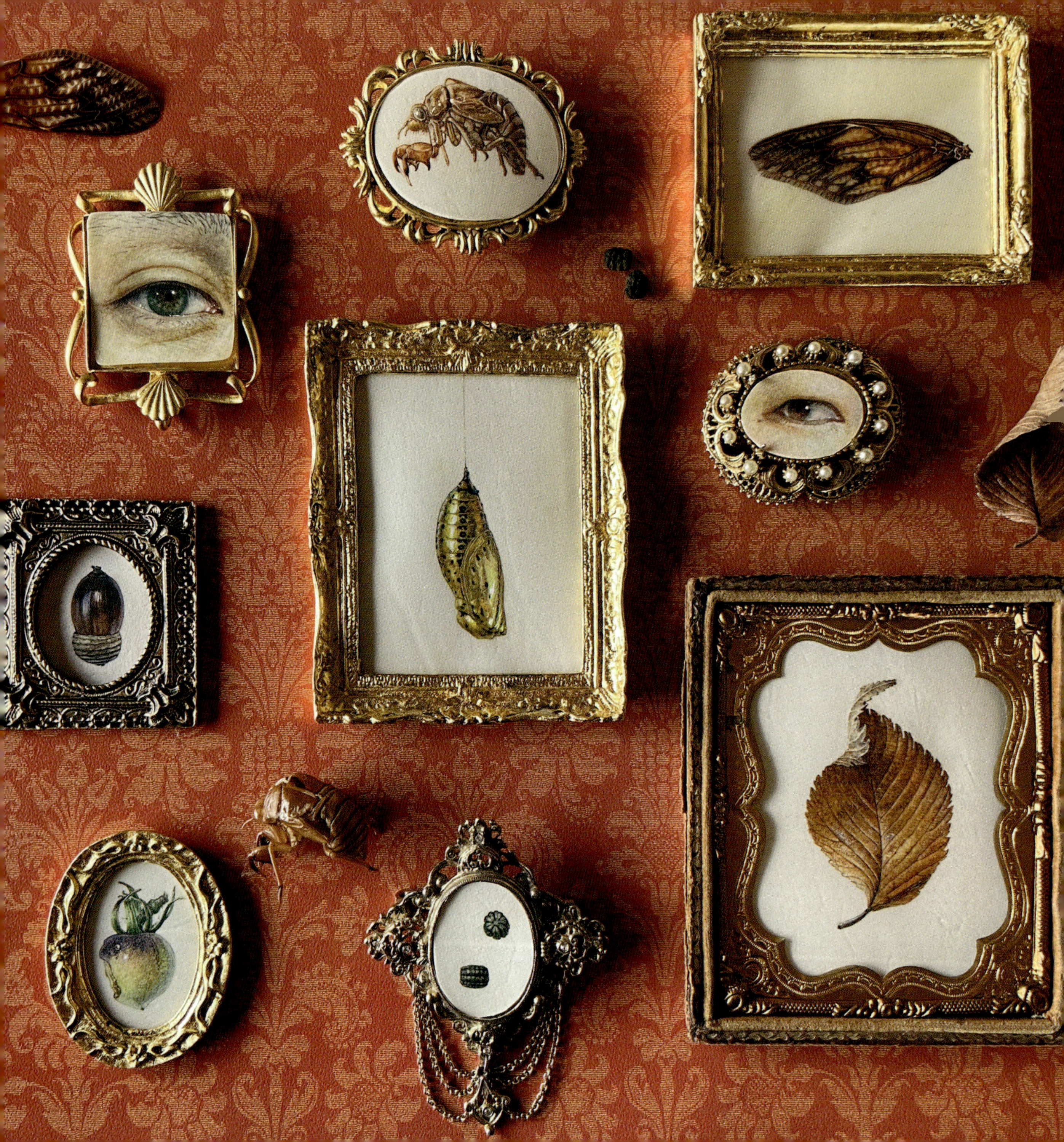

Random curiosities (2016–present)

Pieces of nature (2015–present)
Vellum shreds

In the 16th century, the 'cabinet of curiosities' became popular among aristocrats – private natural history museums, rooms full of collections of natural wonders gathered from all over the world. The trend may have been more about status than science, but it demonstrates that curiosity about the unknown, wild, natural world was stirring.

It was a time when science was not so different from magic, and the collections held questionable objects among the true, exotic treasures. I often think about how confusing and somewhat frightening it must have been to have had no way to confirm what was real and what was not.

But I am attracted to that mixed-up stage in the progression of our understanding of the natural world. The confusion is part of the place I choose to occupy, between serious truth seeker and passionate dreamer. It allows me to ponder, wonder and daydream. Even after decades-worth of research and developments in science, there are still many mysteries and wonders existing in the natural world.

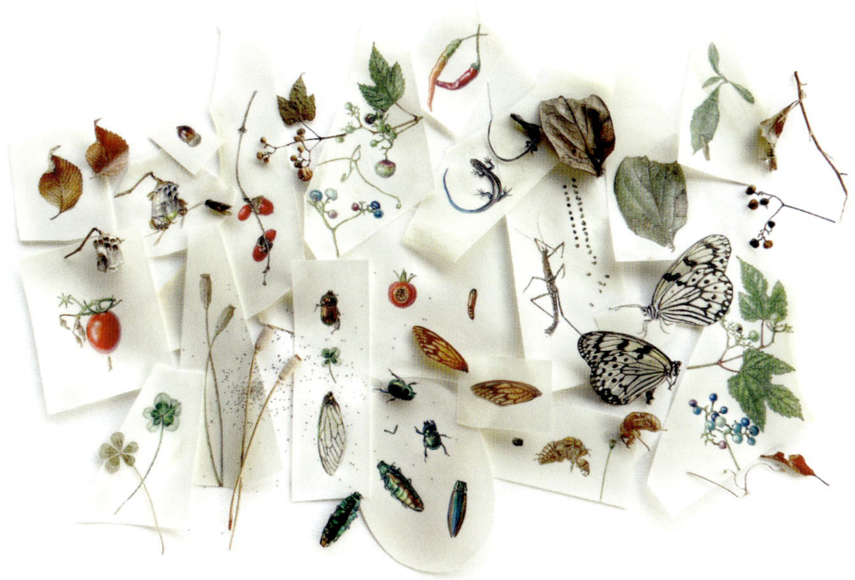

Maple leaves (2017)

Do you have a special collection? What kinds of objects appeal to you?

I think I have had a tendency to be a collector since I was small. My collections were simply hidden gems… treasures to me but to others, worthless objects. Cicada wings, simple acorns and pine cones, cherry blossom petals, unknown tiny red fruits, four-leaf clovers and so on. It was truly exciting when I spotted them during an afternoon walk, and I secretly pocketed them while my guardians looked the other way.

These treasures didn't last long. Half the objects were broken into pieces or crumpled up in my pocket. It brought me huge disappointment when I found them in a bad state when I got home.

The less damaged treasures would be stored in my drawer or my favourite empty cookie tin. But those wouldn't last either. Returning to them later caused more disappointment. The poor objects became dried, shrunken or discoloured and some very unfortunate treasures were covered with mould. That was the end of my collection, so the cookie tin had to be cleared out and sanitised.

At the time, I didn't possess any power to maintain my treasures. So, later in my life, I started to collect them again, this time in the form of painting.

I have been very fortunate to have been invited on artist-in-residence programmes at renowned botanical gardens. Each garden provided me with loads of attractive subjects. Sadly, I had very limited time, especially given my slow pace and countless plants, and several weeks felt very short. So I decided to make a diary, collecting a small piece of a plant each day.

Look at my fabulous collections! Seeing my own collection afterwards, organised neatly in a box, is a blessing, a satisfying moment for any collector. It brings a smile to my lips.

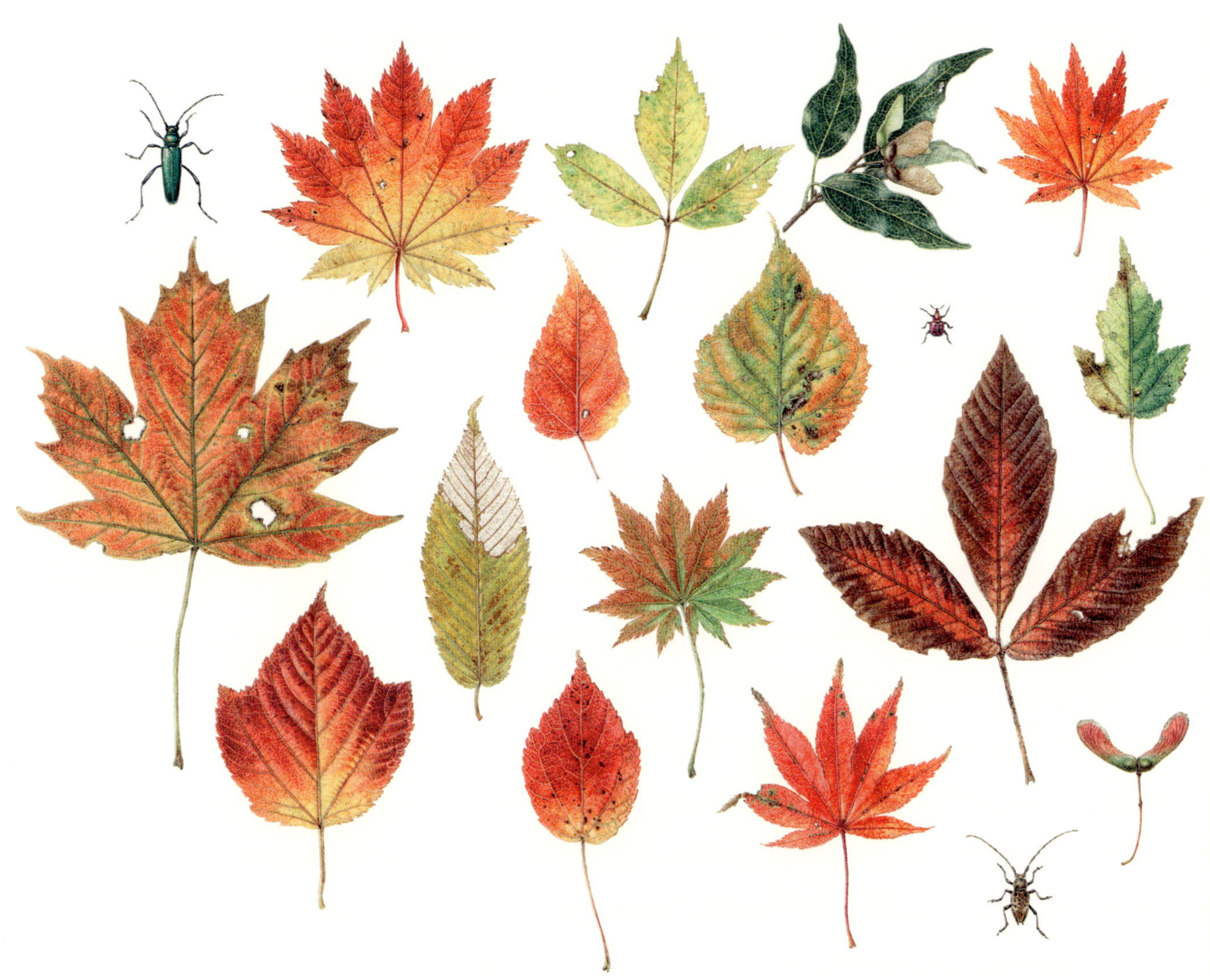

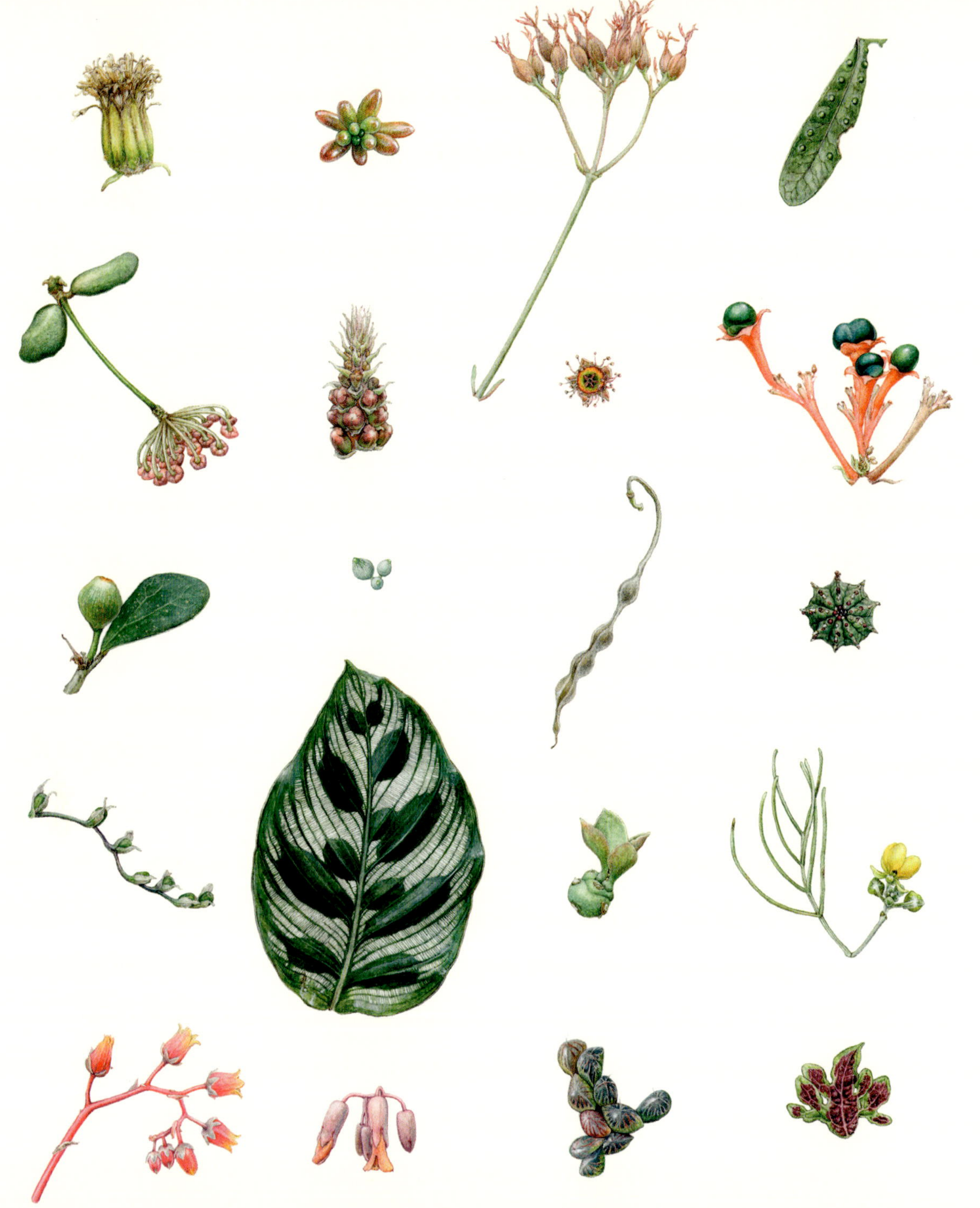

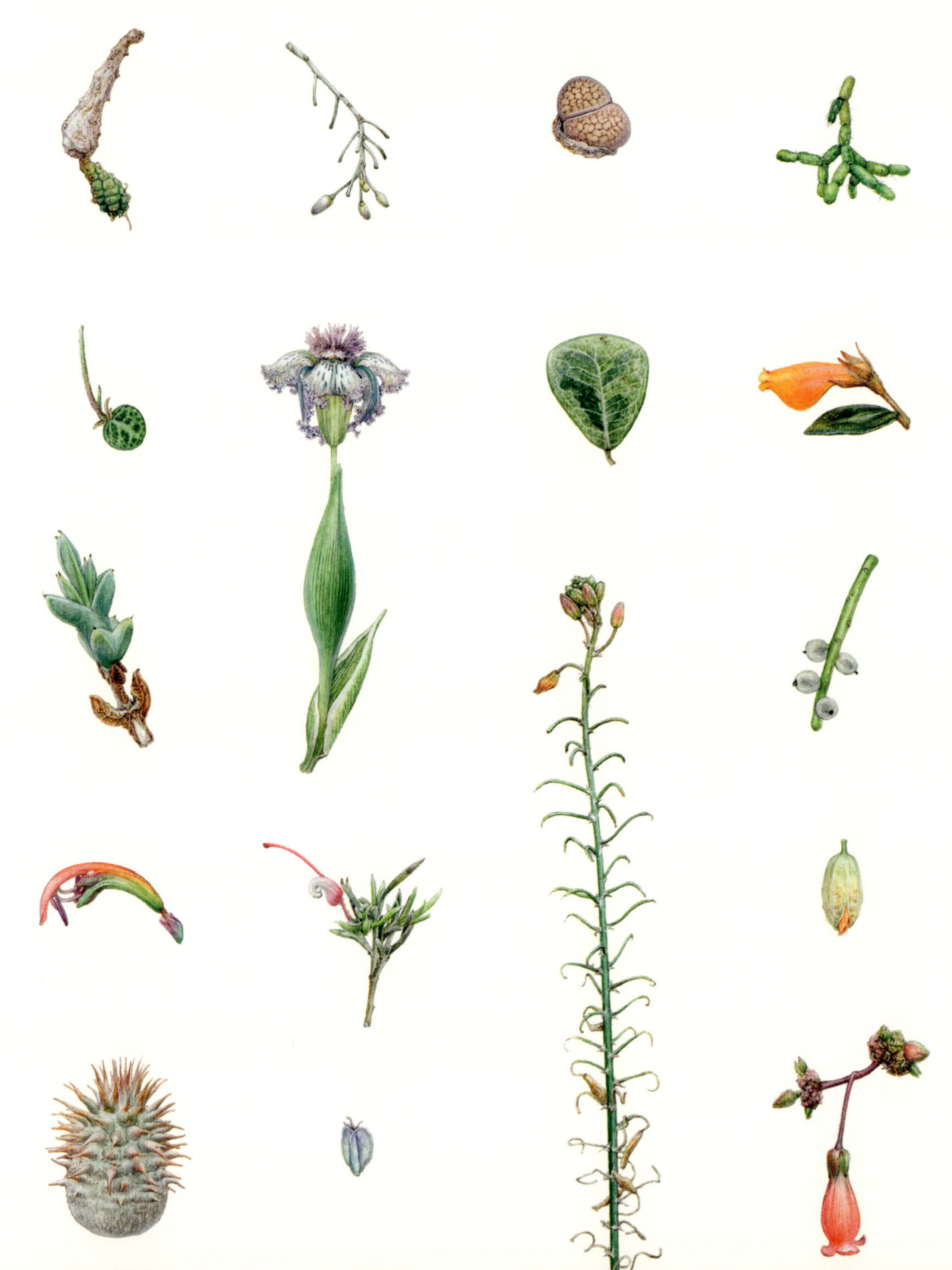

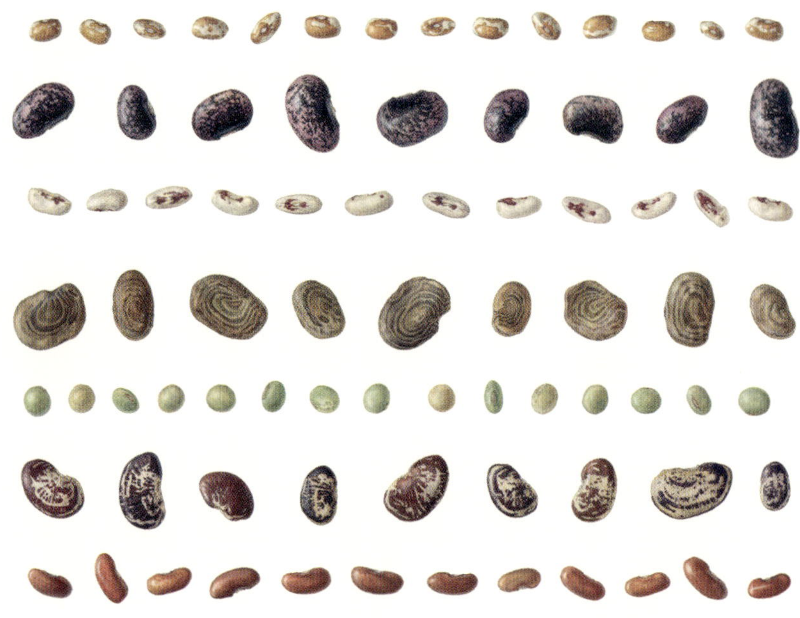

The collection box artworks were composed on a 2.5-inch grid structure. It may not be very obvious since I erased the structure at the end. Without any specific reasons, I thought the 2.5-inch grids were the ideal base to display my collections.

No one, including myself, had ever asked why I picked that structure, but while I was gathering my old memories, two of my favourite things stood out: a periodic table and a chocolate box. Both enchanted me in my youth.

At high school, whenever I felt bored in a classroom, I opened my biology textbook which was full of illustrations. The contents were so captivating

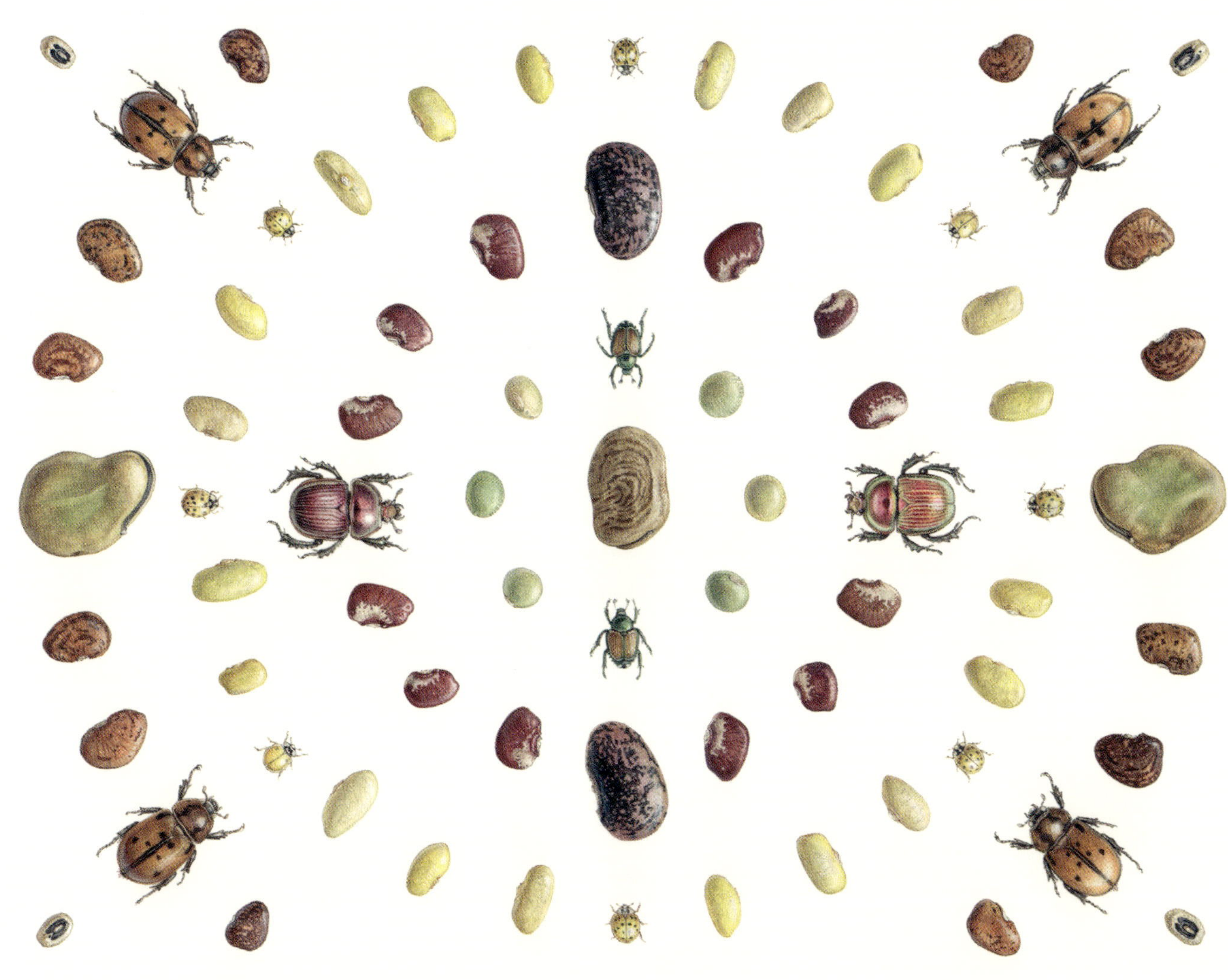

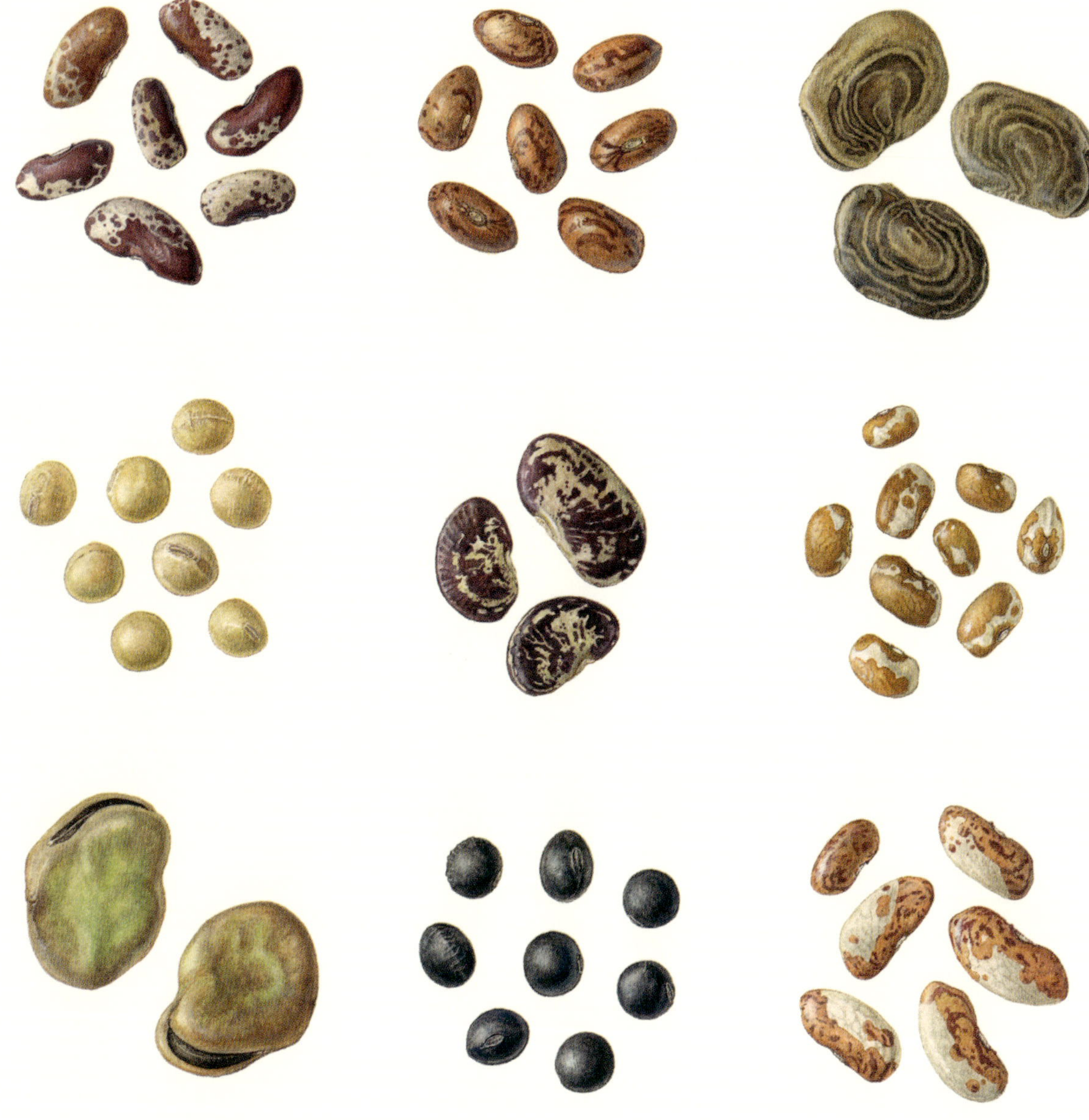

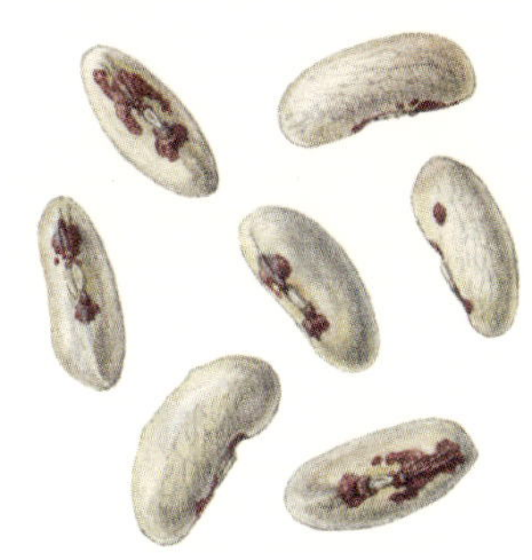

and let me daydream about natural wonders. In a way, that book was one of my early 'cabinets of curiosities'. In it, there was a periodic table which was strangely enchanting. Although the letters in the table were like codes from an unknown world to me, the way all the elements sat neatly in grids attracted me. The element table!

And of course, who doesn't like a box of chocolates? Looking at all the different, decorated chocolates sitting neatly in a grid-partitioned box made my heart throb. It was always such a struggle deciding which one to pick first and I always wished it lasted longer, watching the empty space greedily as if my gaze might bring back a new chocolate.

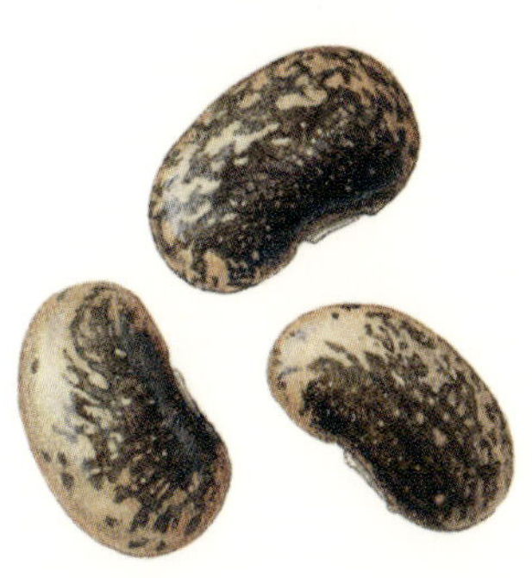

You may think this is backward reasoning and it may be so, but I think recollection works in a strange way. Time moves in one direction, but our memories work more flexibly. I often think memory acts similarly to the key on the glass table in 'Alice in Wonderland'. Do you recall the scene? Alice wants to get smaller to go through a small door. She manages it by drinking a potion, but the door is locked. The door key is laid on the glass table, but shrunken Alice cannot reach it. She wonders if it was there before she took the bottle of potion or whether it popped up from nowhere, later…

I am not sure if the periodic table and box of chocolates were in my mind from the beginning, hinting at me to go ahead with the grid composition, or whether those two favourite things popped into my head later and appeared to make sense.

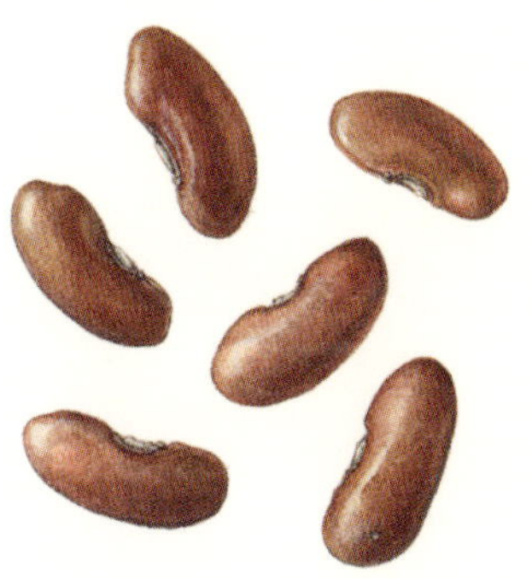

B & B: Grids (2016)

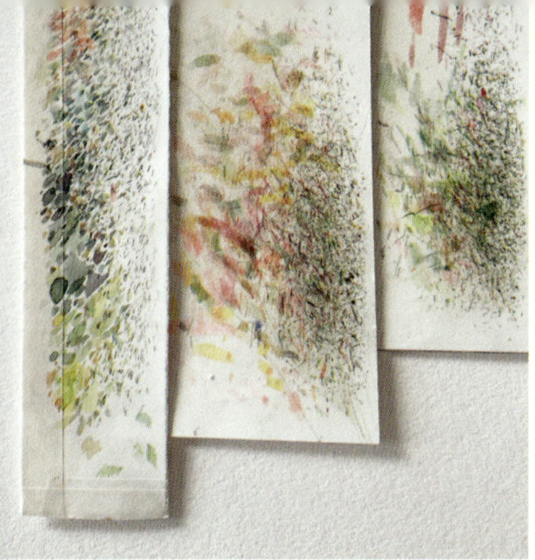
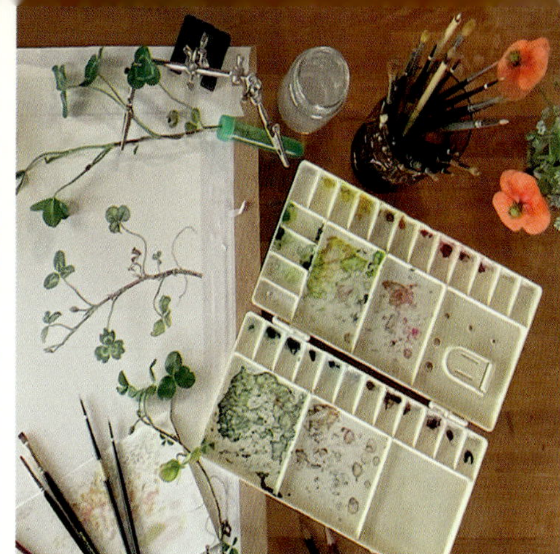
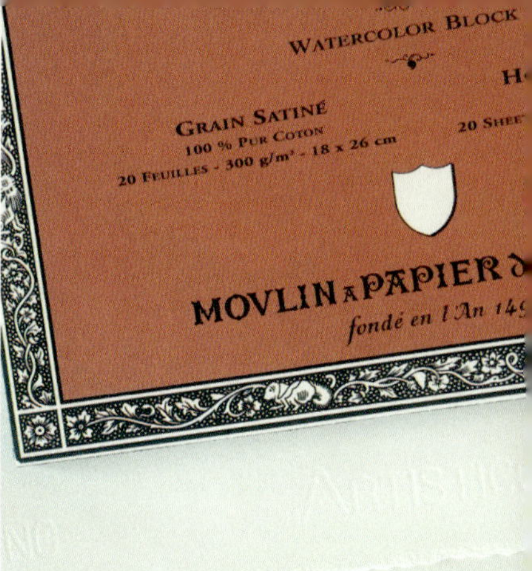

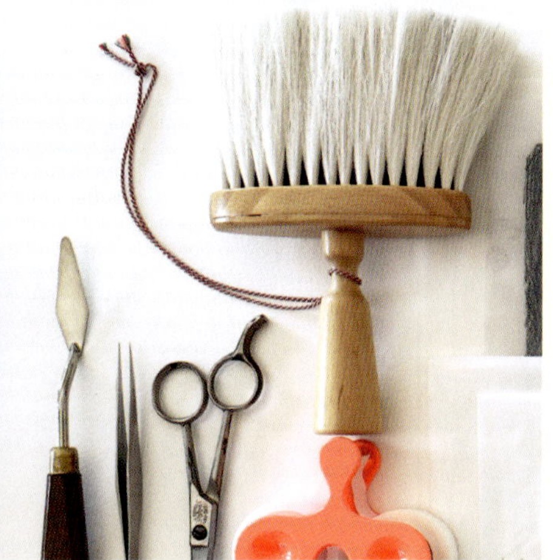

FAQ
Brushes, paper, colour mixing

Throughout my workshops, emails, messages and gallery talks, people always ask me what kind of brushes and paper I use. Oh, I know! These two things are essential.

Another question I often get is, how do I find the right colour? It embarrasses me a little because my answer is, 'I mix constantly'. My way of searching for the right colour is messy.

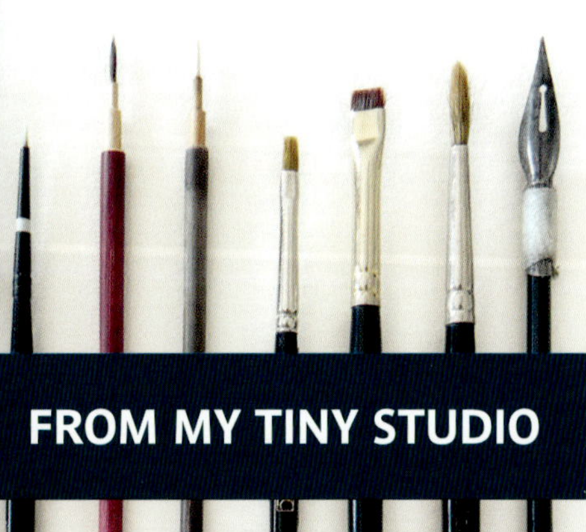

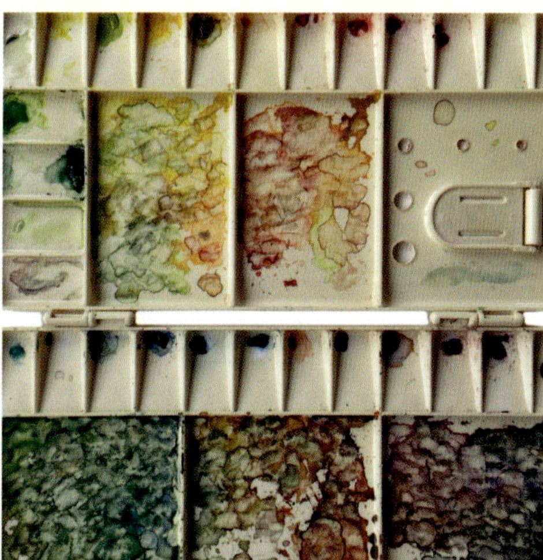

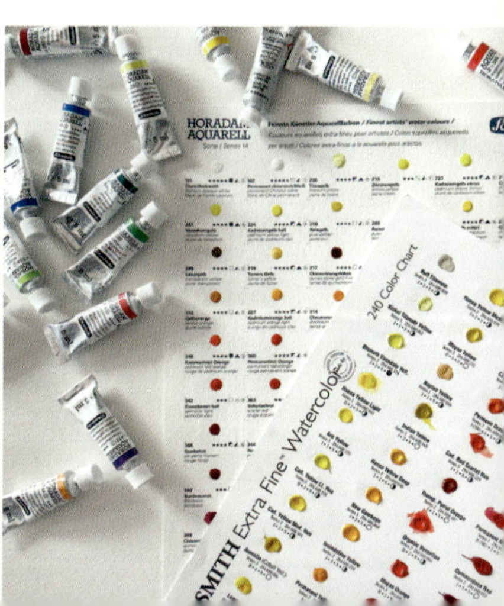

Brushes

Good-for-everything brush

Interlon 1026 Round 0/3 synthetic watercolour brushes are good for everything. Actually, I use this brush almost entirely, even for big subjects. This tiny brush holds an amazing amount of water and allows me to draw thin but long lines in one stroke. The hair is rather hard, but you can create any kind of shade with this brush.

Traditional treasure brush

Makie brushes are traditional handmade brushes made for an Urushi craftsman. These are made from bamboo and cat and mouse hair. Not ordinary bamboo, nor hair from ordinary cats and mice. And these rare materials are not available anymore, so after nine generations making brushes, the craftsman will close his business soon. I was so lucky to be one of the artists who received his last brushes. The brush works best on vellum and it gives me lines thinner than hair. According to legend, Mr Tomitaro Makino drew seven lines in a 1mm width with this brush. I can only draw six lines so far. I am still training.

Colour lifting brush

As well as adding colour, lifting it is also important. It requires a powerful but flexible hair. You need practice to know how much to remove, how much water the brush contains, and how much pressure is needed. I have been doing this for more than three decades and I'm still often surprised.

It is impossible to completely predict how much one stroke will lift the colour from the paper. Right now I'm enjoying those short, middle-sized, flat, synthetic brushes such as Loew-Cornell 7300 shader 2 or 4, or Rosemary & Co. Eradicator small. I keep changing these flat brushes, a firm hair and shaper edge works best with my technique.

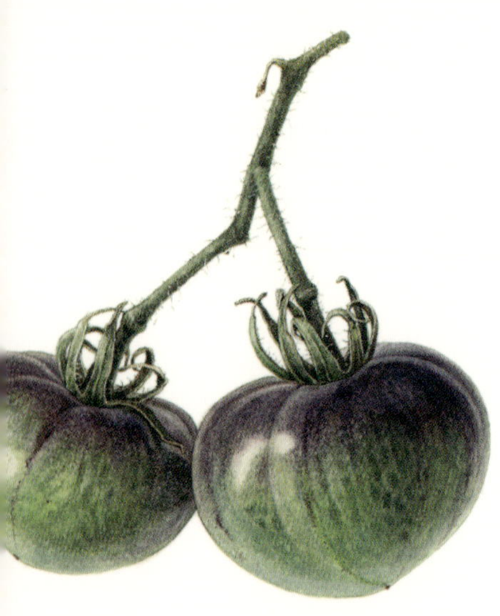

Mixing paint and cleaning palettes brush

I use big round brushes to mix paint or clean palettes. Any bigger round brush will do. Of course, I use them for painting too, but very occasionally.

A nib pen for masking fluid

A nib pen attached to an old brush works well for masking fluid. I use Hunt artists' pens 513EF. Since I'm used to the weight of the Interlon brush handle, I attach the nib to the wrong end of one. This would work with any brush handle you prefer, I think. It works for me!

Paper

For watercolour

Arches hot pressed 300g/m^2 is my favourite paper for watercolour painting–it stays solid after layers and layers of paint. I am not sure how many layers of watercolour I'm going to add until the satisfactory colour emerges and the process includes lifting pigment off the paper too–countless times. Despite the harsh treatment, this paper holds its firmness so I can have a sharp edge.

I use blocks or, if loose paper sheets, I always water-stretch it to a wooden panel.

For coloured pencil

If I'm working with colour pencil, Fabriano Artistico hot pressed 300g/m^2 is the best match. I use Faber Castell Polychromos Colored Pencils.

Twins (Blue tomato, 2016)

Turezure no kusa:
Garden monkshood (2019)

Colour mixing

Colour mixing

As I mentioned, my answer is, 'I mix constantly.' How does that work? Let's say I'm painting a tomato. First, I make a basic tomato skin colour rainbow on a palette (from light yellow orange to deep red, for example) and let it dry. Then I pick the colour closest to what I need for the section I'm working on from the rainbow. If I feel it lacks a greenish tinge, I add a tiny hint of green to the colour and start making a smaller rainbow within it. So, my palette ends up looking like fish scales and each scale is a small rainbow. It may sound complicated, but it's not really. I keep adding and picking up paints and water, so the rainbows on the palette keep shifting and produce for me a very complex colour chart from which I can easily pick the closest subtle shade. Also, I do not expect to get the colour right immediately. On the contrary, I keep adding to the rainbows. Countless layers later, my desired colour slowly emerges.

Colour testing

Testing paper is essential to me. Even though I pick a colour from the palette carefully, it may look different on paper. I am sceptical, like Sherlock Holmes.

Cleaning up

Watercolour is the ideal medium for a lazy person like me. Usually, I do not clean my desk until finishing a work. At the end of the day, I rinse my brushes in a water jar and that's it. I leave everything untouched. Well, maybe I close my pan so as not to get it dusty. The next day, I open the pan and pick up the brush, then simply start working again. No cleaning is involved!

There is one more thing I do, which is to collect the dirty water in a bigger bottle. After a week or so, the pigment falls to the bottom and you can pour the cleaner water down the drain, cleaning up the pigment with a cloth. This way, you minimise contaminating the wastewater with pigment.

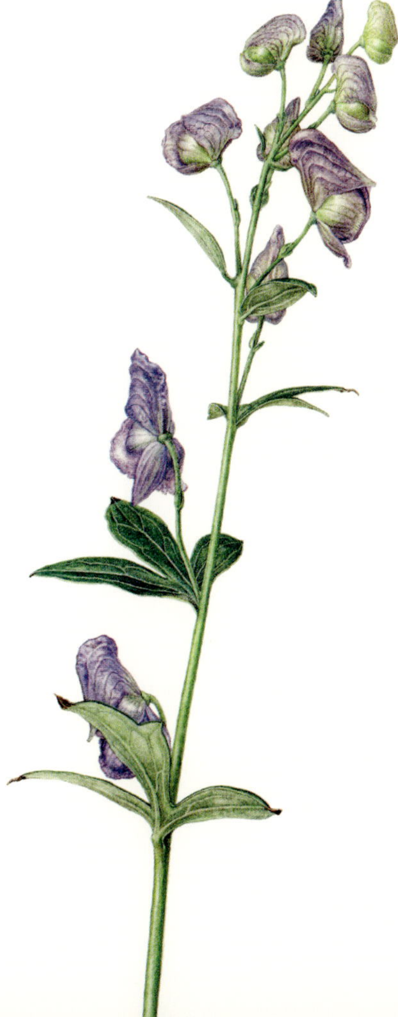

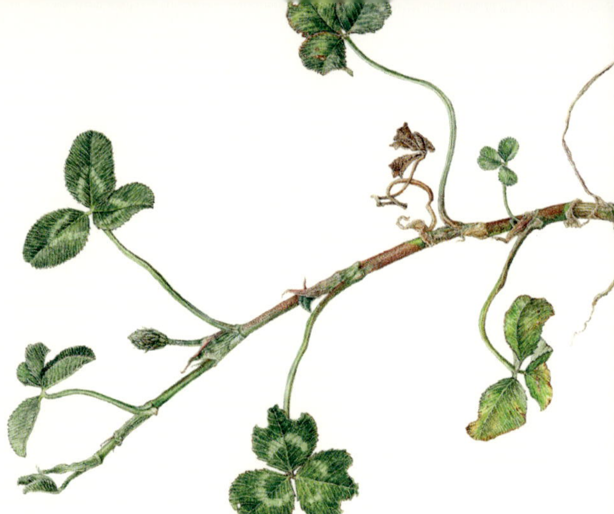

Afterthoughts

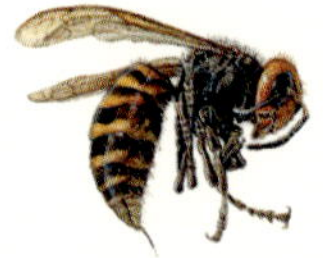

When producing this book, I wasn't sure how to present my artwork. I do care about the composition of the work very much, but the details are the compelling essential piece of what I do. If a whole artwork is printed at book size, all the details cannot be shown. If the image is blown up, the composition of the whole is lost and some parts will be cut out. What should I do?

If I invited you to an exhibition of my work, you could choose to get up-close to see the details or keep your distance to look at the whole composition. How could I make this book as close to that experience as possible? I was going back and forth, wondering how to present the artwork in these limited pages, and decided to focus on the details in the main body of the book but include a list of works as thumbnails of the whole artwork at the back. I hope that this is like handing you a magnifying glass to look at close-ups of the artworks and share the awe I felt when I first saw the details.

Until the day comes when I can show you my actual works and hand you an actual magnifying glass, I hope this book can be your cabinet of curiosities, keeping you amused. My actual artworks will meet you someday, somewhere... until then, a big smile to you.

Asuka

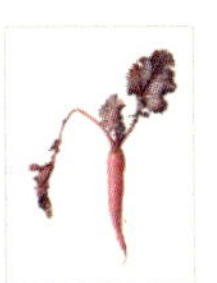

Red daikon (2021)
Watercolour on paper, 12 × 9 in

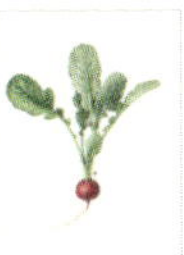

Radish (2018)
Raphanus raphanistrum
subsp. *sativus*
Watercolour on paper, 12 × 9 in

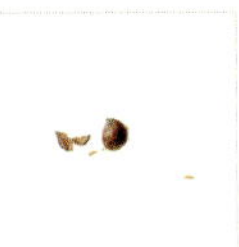

Turezure no kusa:
A chestnut and chestnut worms (2018)
Watercolour on paper, 13¾ × 13¾ in

Turezure no kusa is a series of paintings
inspired by the essay 'Turezuregusa' (徒然草)
by the Japanese monk Yoshida Kenko.

Mimicking his stream-of-consciousness style,
I've attempted to portray the beauty of nature
and transience of life by 'following the brush'.
The collection stands at 45 pieces, all the
same size, and I intend to keep adding to it.

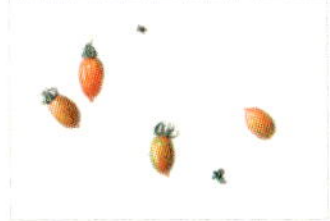

Jewel tomatoes (2022)
Watercolour on paper, 9×13 in

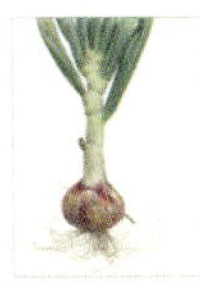

Rainbow Onion (2014)
Allium cepa
Watercolour on paper, 13¼×9 in

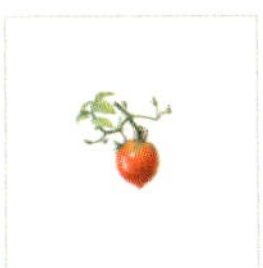

Turezure no kusa:
Breast tomato (2018)
Watercolour on paper, 13¾ ×13¾ in

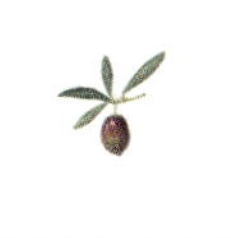

Olive (2018)
Watercolour on paper, 3×3 in

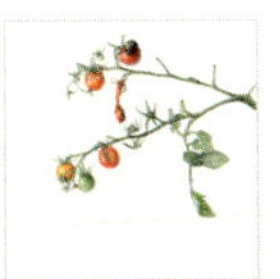

Turezure no kusa:
After long rain tomato (2021)
Watercolour on paper, 13¾ ×13¾ in

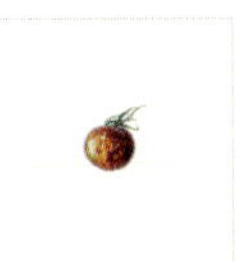

Tiger jewel tomato (2021)
Watercolour on paper, 5×5 in

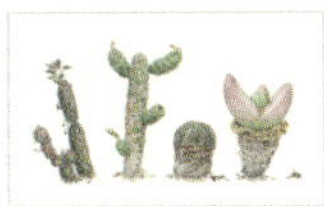

Wave Hill gangsters (2018)
Watercolour on paper, 7½ × 12½ in

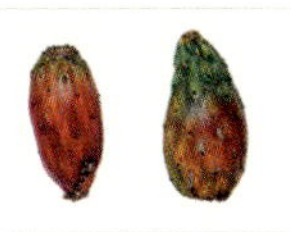

Cactus fruit (Prickly pear cactus, 2012)
Opuntia (unidentified species)
Watercolour on paper, 9 ×13 in

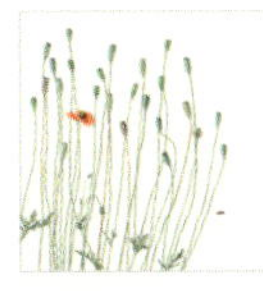

Turezure no kusa:
A big bush of long-headed poppy (2020)
Watercolour on paper, 13¾ ×13¾ in

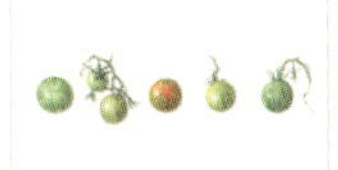

Children's Choir:
Four and a twin zebras (2015)
Watercolour on paper, 8×13½ in

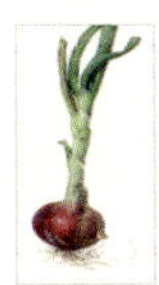

Purple onion (2011)
Allium cepa
Watercolour on paper, 14½ ×10¾ in

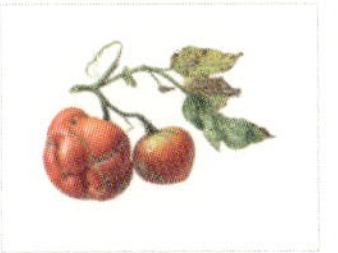

A portrait of a heirloom tomato:
Dancing duo (2015)
Watercolour on paper, 9½×12½ in

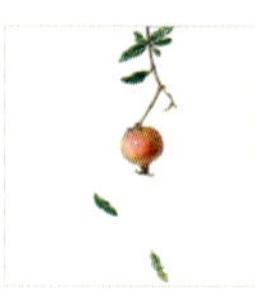

Turezure no kusa:
Pomegranate (2021)
Watercolour on paper, 13¾ × 13¾ in

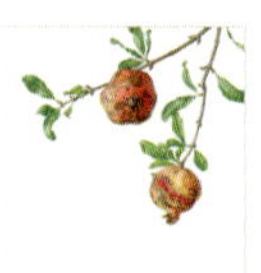

Turezure no kusa:
Pomegranates on a tree (2022)
Watercolour on paper, 13¾ × 13¾ in

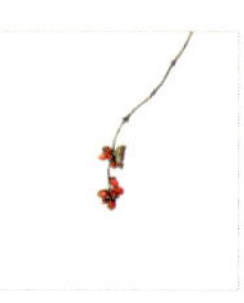

Turezure no kusa:
Red poisonous fruits (2018)
Watercolour on paper, 13¾ × 13¾ in

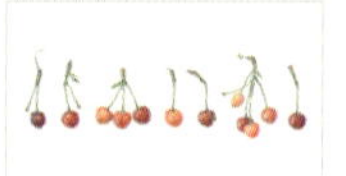

Wild cherry (2018)
Watercolour on paper, 6 × 10½ in

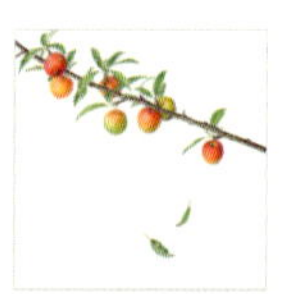

Turezure no kusa:
Plums on a tree (2022)
Watercolour on paper, 13¾ × 13¾ in

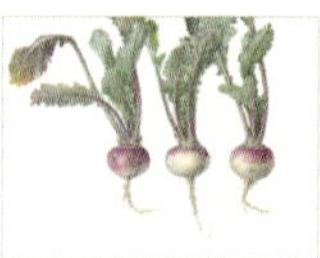

Turnip (Ayameyuki, 2015)
Brassica rapa var. *rapa*
Watercolour on paper, 12 × 16 in

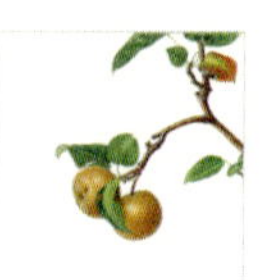

Turezure no kusa
Pears on a tree (2022)
Watercolour on paper, 13¾ × 13¾ in

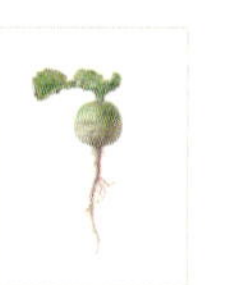

Watermelon radish (2015)
Watercolour on paper, 10 × 7½ in

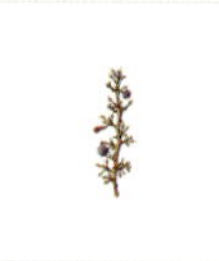

Turezure no kusa:
Grape stem (2018)
Watercolour on paper, 13¾ × 13¾ in

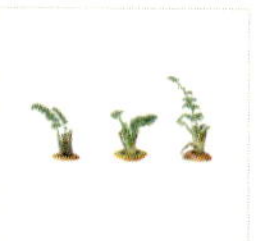

Turezure no kusa:
Three carrot tops (2018)
Watercolour on paper, 13¾ × 13¾ in

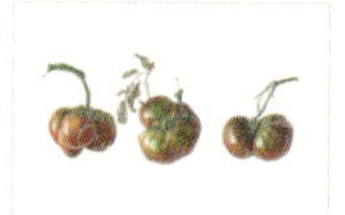

A portrait of a heirloom tomato:
Brandies (2016)
Watercolour on paper, 11 × 15 in

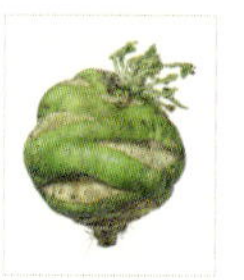

Giant kohlrabi (German turnip, 2012)
Brassica oleracea
Watercolour on paper, 11½ × 9½ in
The Horticultural Society of New York

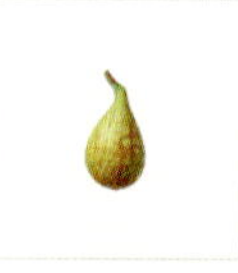

Fig (2020)
Ficus carica
Watercolour on paper, 6⅔ × 6⅔ in

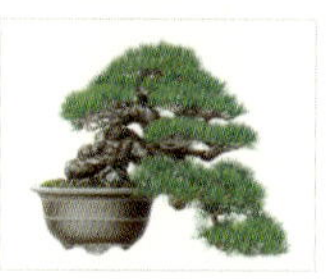

Black Pine Half-cascade-style Bonsai (2015–2017)
Pinus nigra
Oil on paper, 28¼ × 36½ in
The Huntington Library, Art Museum,
and Botanical Gardens

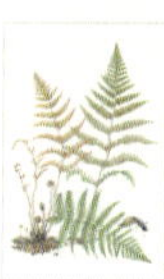

Fern (2013)
Dryopteris erythrosora
Watercolour on paper, 24 × 15½ in
Royal Botanic Gardens, Kew

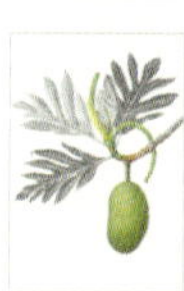

Breadfruit (2019)
Artocarpus altilis
Colour pencil, watercolour and graphite on paper,
15½ × 7½ in
National Tropical Botanical Garden

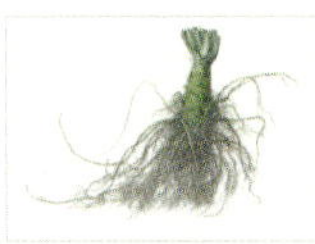

Wasabi (2011)
Eutrema japonicum
Watercolour on paper, 14¾×21¼ in
The Shirley Sherwood Collection

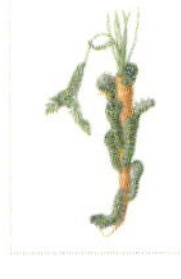

Creep carrot (2013)
Watercolour on paper, 10½ × 7¾ in

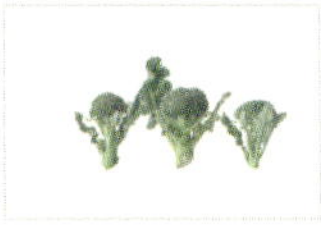

Broccoli (2014)
Brassica oleracea
Watercolour on paper, 7½ × 11½ in

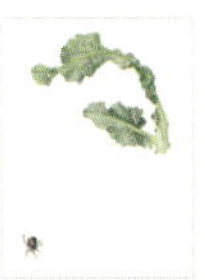

A redback spider, on balance (2015)
Watercolour on paper, 10¾ × 8¼

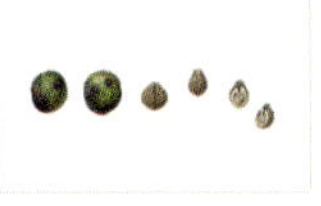

Black walnut (2011)
Juglans nigra
Watercolour on paper, 13½ × 22½ in
The Huntington Library, Art Museum,
and Botanical Gardens

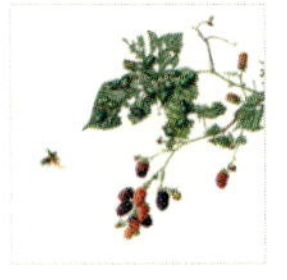

Turezure no kusa:
Blackberry and beetles (2021)
Watercolour on paper, 13¾ ×13¾ in

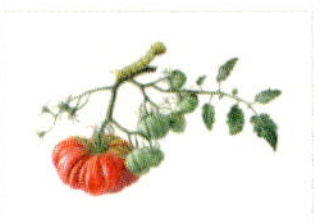

**A portrait of a heirloom tomato:
Pirates (2016)**
Watercolour on paper, 11⅘ × 17⅔ in

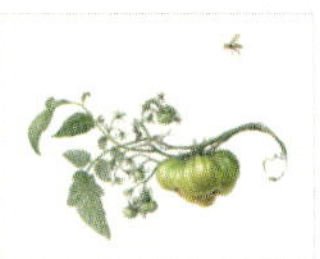

Heirloom tomato (2019–2020)
Animas en el Agua
Watercolour on paper, 10⅔ ×14 in

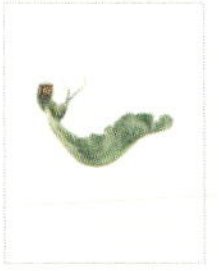

A puss moth caterpillar, on balance (2015)
Watercolour on paper, 9½×7½ in

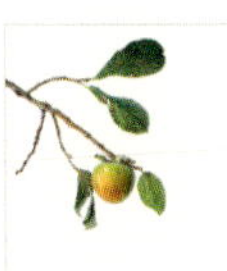

Turezure no kusa:
A persimmon on a tree (2021)
Watercolour on paper, 13¾ ×13¾ in

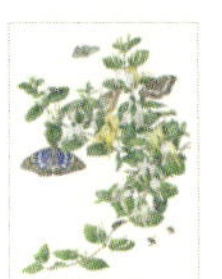

Japanese Honeysuckle (2014)
Lonicera japonica
Watercolour on paper, 17⅖×13⅖ in
The Huntington Library, Art Museum,
and Botanical Gardens

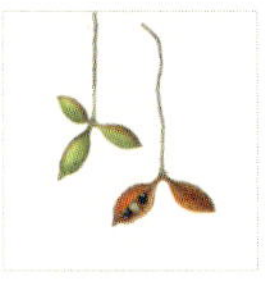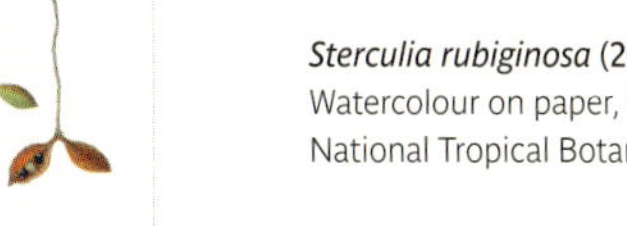

Sterculia rubiginosa (2017)
Watercolour on paper, 8 × 8 in
National Tropical Botanical Garden

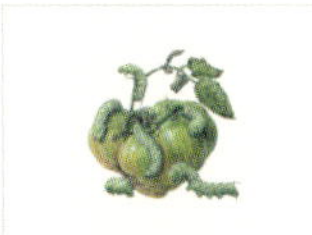

Casanova (2013)
*Solanum lycopersicum,
Manduca quinquemaculata*
Watercolour on paper, 9¼ × 12½ in

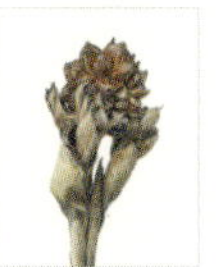

Nipa palm (2018)
Nypa fruticans
Colour pencil and watercolour on paper,
12 × 9⅞ in
National Tropical Botanical Garden

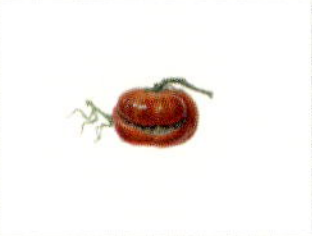

**A portrait of a heirloom tomato:
Peek-a-boo (2022)**
Watercolour on paper, 6⅛ × 8⅞ in

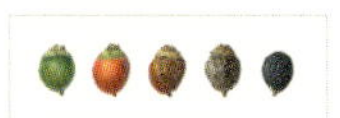

Foxtail palm fruit
Wodyetia bifurcata (2017)
Watercolour on paper, 4½×13½ in

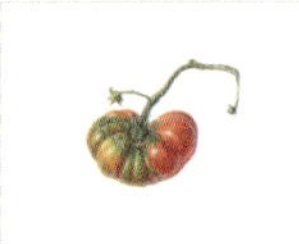

A portrait of a heirloom tomato:
A little pretty pleats (2015)
Watercolour on paper, 7×9 in

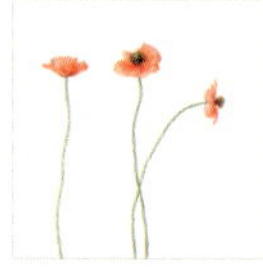

Turezure no kusa:
Three poppies (2021)
Watercolour on paper, 13¾ ×13¾ in

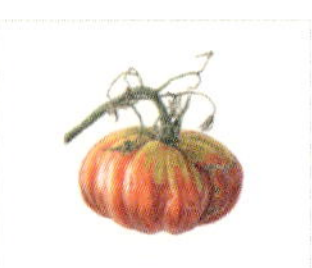

A portrait of a heirloom tomato:
High end magazine senior editor (2016)
Watercolour on paper, 8½ × 10½ in

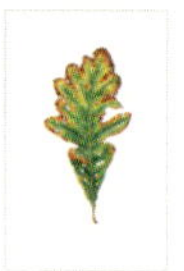

Aged white oak leaf (2021)
Watercolour on paper, 9×5½ in

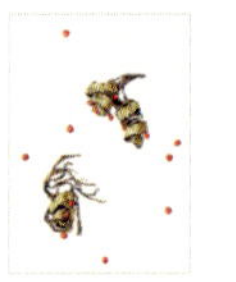

Saga seed pod (2022)
Adenanthera pavonina
Watercolour on paper, 11⅔ × 8½ in
Singapore Botanic Garden, Singapore

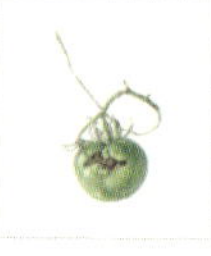

A portrait of a heirloom tomato:
Weeping baby (2015)
Watercolour on paper, 9 × 8 in

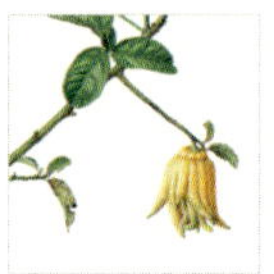

Turezure no kusa:
A Buddha's hand on a tree (2022)
Watercolour on paper, 13¾ ×13¾ in

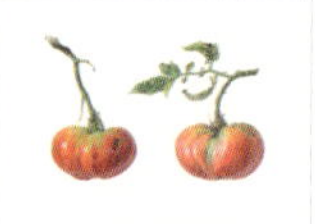

A portrait of a heirloom tomato:
Party girls (2015)
Watercolour on paper, 9 ×12½ in

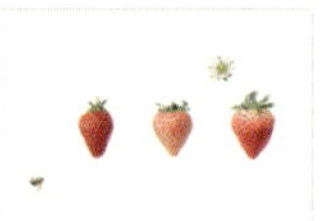

Strawberries, flower,
and a honeybee (2019)
Watercolour on paper, 7 × 10¼ in

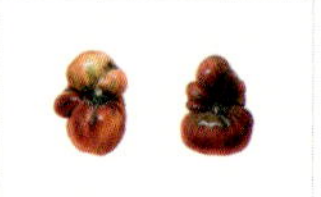

A portrait of a heirloom tomato:
Yakuza brothers (2009)
Watercolour on paper, 11½ ×17½ in

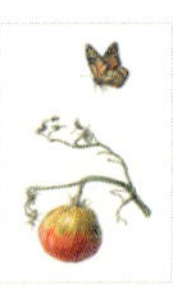

A half-rotten tomato and a butterfly (2018)
Watercolour on paper, 13 × 9 in

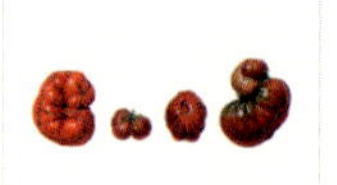

A portrait of a heirloom tomato:
The Smiths (2011)
Watercolour on paper, 13 ×19 in
Hunt Institute

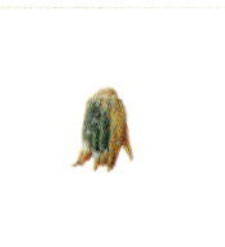

Turezure no kusa:
Mould-covered Buddha's hand (2022)
Watercolour on paper, 13¾ ×13¾ in

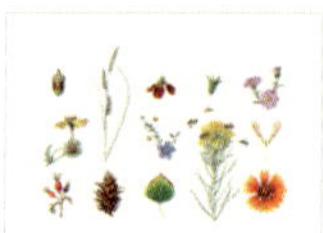

Diary: 2018 Fall Colorado, Denver
12 ×16 in

Turezure no kusa:
Mould-covered plum (2020)
Watercolour on paper, 13¾ ×13¾ in

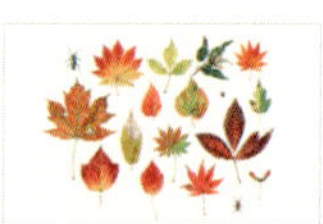

Maple leaves (2017)
Watercolour on paper, 12⅕ × 20 in

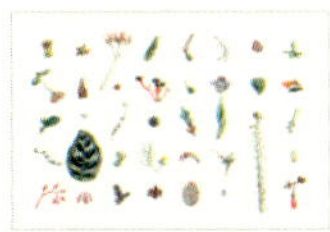

Diary: Wave Hill Conservatory (Winter 2013)
Watercolour on paper, 36 × 24 in

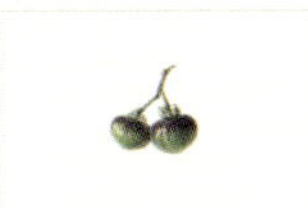

Twins (Blue tomato, 2016)
Watercolour on paper, 5½ × 8½ in

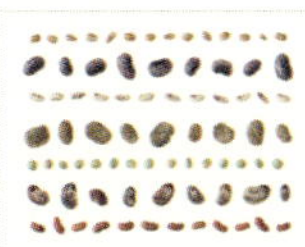

B & B: Horizontal stripes (2016)
Watercolour on paper, 9½ × 12½ in

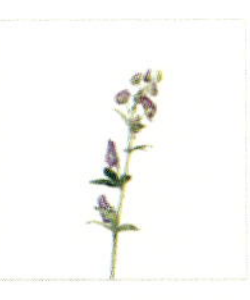

Turezure no kusa:
Garden monkshood (2019)
Watercolour on paper, 13¾ × 13¾ in

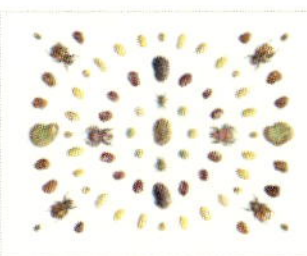

B & B: Multiple circles (2016)
Watercolour on paper, 9½ × 12½ in

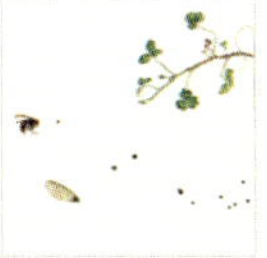

Turezure no kusa:
Treasures found on the ground (2022)
Watercolour on paper, 13¾ × 13¾ in

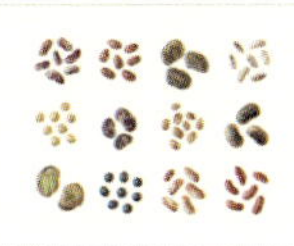

B & B: Grids (2016)
Watercolour on paper, 9½ × 12½ in

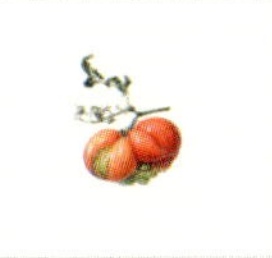

A portrait of a heirloom tomato:
Sexy lady (2021)
Watercolour on paper, 10 × 11½ in

Two Rivers Press has been publishing in and about Reading
since 1994. Founded by the artist Peter Hay (1951–2003), the press
continues to delight readers, local and further afield, with its varied list
of individually designed, thought-provoking books.

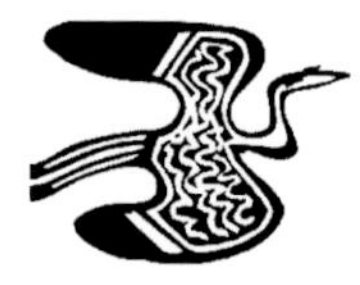